"We live in a sex-obsessed culture, so the notion of single women living fulfilled, joyful and celibate lives is totally counter-cultural, and hugely challenging. Andrea encourages us to take God's word seriously and meet that challenge head on. Her honesty, humour and wisdom will challenge the way you think, warm your heart, and nourish your soul—which is exactly what happened when I read this book. This is not just for single women; everyone should read it to understand the pressures on single women, the mistakes others can make, and how church families can be truly encouraging. Worth the asking price for chapter seven alone."
Rev Carrie Sandom, associate minister for women, St John's Tunbridge Wells, Kent, UK; author of "Different By Design"

"This is not just another book on singleness. It will help you to know wholehearted contentment, and see singleness as a true gift. A brilliant book."
Dr Helen Roseveare, missionary, conference speaker and author

"*The* most helpful and biblical book I have read on singleness. Most others made me mad or sad, but this made me rejoice. Andrea helps us lift our eyes from our situation and gaze upon Jesus, who loves us and delights in us."
Rev Caroline West, curate, St Mary's Basingstoke, Hampshire, UK; lecturer at Cornhill Training Course, London

"Most women regard the idea of singleness with horror, not a gift to be wanted, and certainly never good. Andrea Trevenna confronts this reality head on, with an honest look at what this says about our hearts. Full of biblical wisdom, this book truly shows how to be single and satisfied."
Dr Kirsten Birkett, tutor in ethics and philosophy at Oak Hill Theological College, London; author of "The Essence of Feminism"

"Among a shelf of books on singleness, this one stands out because it deals with our hearts. Andrea encourages us with the great news that if we get our hearts right, then we really can have the satisfaction we all yearn for. I'll be encouraging others to read this book and praying that their lives will be changed as they allow God to change their hearts."
Rosie Dunn, London Women's Convention Committee

"I really appreciate this book, and I will keep coming back to it. Andrea is very honest about what being a single woman is like, and she points us to the real change that Christ brings to our everyday lives. I really enjoyed the down-to-earth examples and the chatty and engaging style, as well as the food for thought throughout the book. I highly recommend it."
Annabel Heywood, Parish and Women's Worker, St Ebbe's Oxford, UK.

The heart of singleness

How to be single and satisfied

Andrea Trevenna

To my parents, John and Eileen,
with heartfelt thanks for your constant love,
encouragement, prayers and friendship

The heart of singleness: *How to be single and satisfied*
© Andrea Trevenna/The Good Book Company, 2013

Published by
The Good Book Company
Tel (UK): 0333 123 0880;
International: +44 (0) 208 942 0880
Email: info@thegoodbook.co.uk

Websites:
UK: www.thegoodbook.co.uk
North America: www.thegoodbook.com
Australia: www.thegoodbook.com.au
New Zealand: www.thegoodbook.co.nz

Unless indicated, all Scripture references are taken from the HOLY BIBLE,
NEW INTERNATIONAL VERSION. Copyright © 2011 International Bible
Society. Used by permission.

ISBN: 9781908762856

Printed and bound by CPI Group (UK) Ltd, Croydon, CR0 4YY
Design by André Parker

Contents

1. The *gift* of singleness?!

What is the worst thing that could possibly happen to you in life?

My answer: staying single.

Or at least, that's how I'd have answered when I was 18, and for a good few years after that. I couldn't think of anything worse than being a "Miss" for ever. Never having any rings on that one crucial finger on my left hand, never introducing people to my "significant other"—that was as bad as it could get.

I'm 42 now, and I'm still single. There have been many times, since I was 18, when that has been really painful, when being single has made me cry, when I have thought that God has surely made a mistake. I still have days when being single is a struggle, especially when I go somewhere new on my own and someone asks me who my husband is, or how many children I have.

You may not go so far as to think that being single is the worst thing that could possibly happen to you, as 18-year-old me did. But if you are a single woman reading this, it's probably not something that you've chosen to be. It's not what you dreamed of when you were young. You'll know that feeling inside that whispers: *It wasn't meant to be like this.*

You complete me

And that feeling is reinforced by our culture. Love is (to steal a song title) all around us: we are bombarded daily with all sorts of wisdom on how to find, get and keep the man* of our dreams.

Just turning on the radio reminds us of this. While making a cup of tea just now, "Don't you want me baby?" by The Human League and "All you need is love" by The Beatles were playing on the radio (I was clearly not listening to the current top 20!). The vast majority of today's hits seem to be about relationships, love or the heart. They're about longing for a love you don't have, or about finding a love you long for, or being rejected by the one you love, or losing the love you once had.

All you need is love—all you need is a lover. That's why, over the last few years, there has been a massive surge in the number of online dating agencies available to help you find him. There are literally millions of them on offer. When I googled "dating agencies", over 44 million hits came up. "Christian dating agencies" gave me 2 million options.

Most of those sites will tell you that the fairy tales we grew up with, and the romantic comedies we watch, are true. They'll assure you that in life, the boy and the girl always end up together... and always live happily ever after. Even if (in fact especially if) the two main characters start off absolutely hating each other, you can guarantee it will end in true love.

---

* It may be that, for you, you find yourself attracted to finding "her", rather than "him". If this is you, then you might like to read Emily's story, in the "Real Faith" section on page 97. This book isn't the place for going into what the Bible says about homosexuality. But that doesn't mean it won't be helpful for you to read, because all single women, no matter who we feel attracted to, find our deepest desires are met only by one person—Jesus. If you want to think about what the Bible says about same-sex attraction, a good place to start is *Is God Anti-Gay?* by Sam Allberry (www.thegoodbook.co.uk/ssa or ...com/ssa).

Happy endings mean a couple ending up in love. And we just love those happy endings because, I guess, that's what we're all hoping for. So if that's not the ending in my life, or your life, surely something's gone wrong.

If you've seen the Tom Cruise film *Jerry Maguire* (between this and my music tastes, I'm beginning to show my age), you'll probably remember the line at the end of the film when Tom says to Dorothy Boyd, played by Renee Zellweger: "You complete me". If we're single, the chances are that deep down we long to hear someone (and it doesn't need to be Tom Cruise) say that to us.

Our culture says we need "the one", and that we're right to feel incomplete until we find him.

Made for each other

And, in many ways, the Bible says that our feelings and our culture are right.

We were made to live in loving relationships. Love and marriage were invented by a loving God as part of his perfect world. Seeing them as things to be highly valued is a right instinct (though our culture, and even our feelings, can twist and spoil love and relationships until they're not good for us at all).

After all, Tom Cruise wasn't the first man to feel incomplete until he found his girl. Right at the beginning of the Bible, having made the first man, God says:

> It is not good for the man to be alone. I will make a helper
> suitable for him. (Genesis 2 v 18)

So God makes the first woman out of the man's rib. She's made from him, and in a sense is made for him. This couple really could say: "We were made for each other".

The man is overjoyed! And Genesis continues:

> That is why a man leaves his father and mother and is united
> to his wife, and they become one flesh. (v 24)

They are perfect for each other, and are given to each other in marriage. It is not good for humans to be alone. It is very good for them to be in love, married, and each other.

And Genesis 2 sets the tone for the rest of the Bible. So when I feel that being single is awful, that something has gone wrong, that finding a man is what I most need... God agrees, doesn't he? Marriage is good: singleness is bad, right?

Better?

Not quite. Yes, God made marriage to be great—and if you long to be married, that feeling is not wrong. Yet here's a verse that as a single woman I need to hear, but which actually I'd often rather not hear:

> To the unmarried and the widows I say: it is good for them to
> stay unmarried, as I do.   (1 Corinthians 7 v 8)

The writer is Paul, an apostle chosen by Jesus Christ to teach his church and write his word. His words are God's words. And he says it is good to be single. Not just OK, tolerable, bearable. Good.

How do you feel about that?

It's not that Paul's made a slip of the pen here. In 1 Corinthians 7, he looks at a number of different singleness scenarios: at those who have never been married, those who have been widowed, and those who are engaged. And over and over again he seems to say: Marriage good: singleness *better*. See what you make of what he says...

It is good for a man not to marry but since there is so much immorality, each man should have his own wife, and each woman her own husband. (v 1-2, NIV 84)

I wish that all of you were as I am [ie: single]. But each of you has your own gift from God; one has this gift, another has that. (v 7)

Are you unmarried? Do not look for a wife [or husband].
(v 27, NIV84).

Those who marry will face many troubles in this life, and I want to spare you this. (v 28)

A woman is bound to her husband as long as he lives. But if her husband dies, she is free to marry anyone she wishes, but he must belong to the Lord. In my judgment, she is happier if she stays as she is. (v 39-40)

Being single is a gift (v 7)—a present from God. Paul says it leaves us "happier" (v 40). It's marriage, not singleness, that brings "many troubles" (v 28). So if we're not married right now, then we're currently enjoying this "gift" from God—experiencing the "happiness" of singleness.

As you read God's words in 1 Corinthians 7, how do you react? "Singleness means less trouble than marriage? I'll take the trouble!" "Singleness is happier? I don't want that sort of happiness!"

"Singleness is good? Not for me. That's simply wrong."

The unwanted gift

I guess we could call singleness, in most cases, the unwanted gift. I once saw a book titled: *If singleness is a gift, what's the return policy?*, which pretty much sums up how many of us feel about our singleness. If you're reading this and you're not a Christian, the idea that being single is a gift probably sounds crazy. And if you're reading this and you are a Christian, then it probably sounds, well, crazy.

It's not easy to be grateful for a gift that you don't want, to enjoy a present that is totally not what you asked for. One Christmas, when my sister and I were 6 and 8, our parents gave us a train set for Christmas. It was a very nice train set, a state-of-the-art Hornby train set... but it was a train set! This was not what I wanted at all. I wanted a Tiny Tears doll. (Looking back on that Christmas, I asked my mum recently if she thought my dad had wanted a son. She replied: "No, but he did want a train set!")

My father is wonderful. But that Christmas, he didn't give me what I wanted, what was good. His idea of a good gift didn't match up with mine.

Is God like that? How can singleness possibly be a good gift? Surely Paul (and God) must have got this wrong, we think. We may not think it in our heads—if we're Christians, we know that God's word is God's word, that it's all true and right and good—but we feel it in our hearts. And, normally, it's what happens in my heart that directs what happens in my life.

How on earth can anyone really, really believe in their heart that being a single Christian (that is, not "being single" so I can sleep around, but rather, not sleeping around because I'm single) is better?

The heart of singleness

So this is a book about our hearts. It's about what's going on in our hearts as we think about singleness. It's not a book full of doctrine; it isn't mean to be the last word on the whole issue;

and I certainly don't have all the answers. My aim is to help us to look at our hearts, to look at our dreams and loves and hopes and fears about singleness in the light of God's word.

You may be reading this book as a Christian, or as someone who hasn't worked out what they think about Jesus Christ. You may be single having never been married; you may have been married but now be single again, through divorce or bereavement. You may have been unmarried and sexually active in the past, either as a Christian or before you became a Christian, and find it hard to be single, celibate and satisfied now.

You may be young and single, and deep down assuming this won't last for much longer; you may be a little older, and deep down realising that this might continue through your whole life. You may have been heartbroken in a previous relationship, or abused as a child or an adult (in which case, let me say at the start that the contents of this short book won't be all you need. I hope it'll be really helpful for you—but do speak to a trusted Christian friend, or pastor, about your particular circumstances). Or you may be married, but wanting to help and support single friends.

Our circumstances will be very different; your past and your present may not be like mine, and not all the experiences I talk about in this book will be ones you've been through. And at the back of the book, you can read about some other women's lives, and about their joys and struggles as they deal with singleness in very different circumstances.

But in the end, whatever our situation, fundamentally our hearts are pretty much all the same. So if we're single, we'll all at times struggle with the same feelings, and all at times be attracted to the same apparent solutions. And ultimately, as we'll see, our heart's longings are all actually met at the same place.

It can be quite uncomfortable looking at our own hearts. But it will (I hope) be liberating and exciting, too. So as we begin, take some time to think through these questions:

- How is your heart? What are you feeling about singleness?

- Are you struggling with being single? Are you feeling angry and bitter and resentful towards God? Do you feel he has let you down, forgotten you, given you second-best? Have you turned your back on him altogether?

- Are you gritting you teeth and getting on with it? Or determined to change it? Or generally fine with it, but experiencing the odd moment of doubt?

- Are you assuming if you live with it now, then God will give you what you really need later on?

- What did you feel in your heart when you read those verses about your singleness being a good gift from God, one that you can welcome?

I think that instinctively our hearts tell us God is wrong, even if our heads know that he is always right. But here's the thing: wouldn't it be great if, somehow, God were right? If there were a way for singleness not to be at best a quiet regret, at worst a personal tragedy?

There is. Our hearts can change. It's possible to view singleness as a blessing, a gift, even if we haven't chosen it. It's possible to enjoy a contentment that isn't based on our relationship status, and isn't affected by it.

It's possible to be single, and satisfied. That's what this short book is about. My prayer is that as you read it, you will come to truly believe and experience that too—not only in your head, but in your heart as well.

2. Finding a man

Do you ever imagine the man of your dreams?

What's he like? What do you look for or long for in a husband, in those moments when you let your mind wander? My ideal would be kind, supportive, protective, patient, understanding, affirming, trustworthy, capable and steady (basically, though it sounds a bit clichéd, Mr Darcy from *Pride and Prejudice*).

I have actually met a few such men in my life; men who were everything I had hoped they would be—strong yet sensitive, responsible yet fun. They were just what I had longed for. They were amazing men.

And then I got to know them.

I had admired them and assessed them from afar. I had thought I knew them, and that they were a twenty-first century Mr Darcy. But the more time I spent with them, and the closer I got to them, the more I realised that, although they had many great qualities, they were in fact far from the perfect men I had imagined them to be. And no doubt they were going through the same re-appraisal of me, too. (In fact, I know they were—one of them once told me!)

Looking back now, I can see that I had hugely unfair and unrealistic expectations. No man could have ever lived up to my standards. I must have heard too many fairy tales as I was growing up. Fairy stories don't generally focus on the pressures and realities of day to day life, and tend to set the bar pretty high for guys (after all, in the land of Far Far Away, the men are usually princes!).

I'm not for a moment saying that having unrealistic expectations is always (or often) why single women are single. Many single women have much more realistic dreams when it comes to a husband than I did; and Mr Darcy may be nothing like your dreams. Maybe your idea of a perfect husband is simply a nice, ordinary guy who loves you well.

The Bible tells us that the longing for a perfect husband is, in fact, God-given; and that it can be fulfilled. And it tells us that this longing can be met whether we are married or single.

The relationship we were made for

In the Old Testament book of Jeremiah, God describes his relationship with his people, the nation of Israel. But he doesn't talk about it being a relationship between "Creator" and "creatures", or even "God" and "my people". He pictures his relationship with them in a very striking, and much more intimate, way:

> I remember the devotion of your youth, how as a bride you
> loved me and followed me through the wilderness, through
> a land not sown. Israel was holy to the LORD, the firstfruits
> of his harvest; all who devoured her were held guilty, and
> disaster overtook them," declares the LORD ... "I brought you
> into a fertile land to eat its fruit and rich produce.
>
> (Jeremiah 2 v 2-3, 7a)

God uses an image of his people as a bride; his bride.

The nation of Israel is his special, chosen people. Of all the surrounding nations, he has chosen her to be his. And he hasn't just chosen her, he has protected her, led her to a lush land of her own, and provided for her every need.

Israel's "husband", the eternal creator God, was perfect; so he could perfectly meet her deepest longings. Again and again, we see that God has a husband's heart:

> I will betroth you to me for ever; I will betroth you in
> righteousness and justice, in love and compassion. I will
> betroth you in faithfulness.   (Hosea 2 v 19-20)

God was a husband who always did the right thing, the good thing, the loving and thoughtful thing. He gave his bride all they needed, and more; he "gave her the grain, the new wine and oil, [and] lavished on her the silver and gold" (v 8). Israel wanted for nothing. God was never less than the perfect husband. There was no disappointment, no flaws from up close.

Israel had been totally bowled over by how unworthy and helpless she was, and how wonderfully good and holy and loving her God was. There was a humility in her that came from knowing that she had been nothing but a helpless and hopeless slave in Egypt, and that God had rescued her. He, as it were, had knelt down to her as she sat in the dirt, lifted her downcast head, picked her up and brought her to himself.

And he hadn't done that because she was some kind of supermodel among the nations, and so of course a great God would pick her. No, she was a slave! It's like in the films where the geeky girl, rather than the stunning, popular cheerleader gets chosen by the high school football captain.

But as well as this humility, there was also a right dignity in the people of Israel at their amazing status—being in relationship with the living God who had made them to be his. Israel knew who she was, as a people, because she knew whose she was. She had purpose, significance and security because she was God's bride.

This is the relationship she was made for. This was where her deepest longings were satisfied.

Delight and devotion

If you've ever spent time with the average newly-married bride, you will have a good idea of what delighted devotion looks like. The bride gazes at her husband, hanging on his every word, her hand permanently on his knee or on his arm, glowing with happiness. She radiates an unmistakably proud glow at the fact that she is "his wife"! There is total commitment and adoration.

Often, new brides seem to be totally unaware of everyone else around them. They are lost in their husbands, talking and thinking about nothing else. (At this point in the relationship, the bride's friends, particularly the single ones, require a lot of patience!) They long to be with their husband, and can't bear to be apart from him.

Of course, actions speak louder than words. So a bride doesn't just say: "I love you". She shows: "I love you", too. So she cooks what she knows her husband really likes; she gets up at 5am to go and meet him at the airport; she stops what she's doing to listen to a problem he's facing, and gives her time to thoughtfully giving the best advice she can. And she doesn't do any of that because she has to, but because she wants to.

That's the kind of delighted devotion Israel had for her God. She looked to him, followed him, trusted and obeyed him. She listened to him; she marvelled at all that he had done for her; she delighted in him. She delighted in being his. It's all summed up in five wonderful words in the book of Isaiah: "Your Maker is your husband" (54 v 5).

I really love you

I was at a silver wedding anniversary party recently. It was a wonderful celebration in a beautiful garden on a gorgeous sunny day, with great food and good friends. But the real highlight of the day for me was the speech the husband made about (or rather, to) his wife. The speech culminated in him gazing at her and saying: "Jeanette, I really love you".

At that moment, among all the joy and happiness I felt for them, there was a slight pang. I thought: "I would love a husband to look into *my* eyes and say those words to *me*: 'Andrea, I really love you'."

Well, God has.

God rescued a people from hopelessness and brought them into relationship with him. And God rescues individuals, too— helpless individuals who are looking for relief from the pain in their hearts; disappointed individuals who have been looking for that relief in all the wrong places, and have never found what they were longing for.

Just another man?

In John's account of Jesus' life, he recounts the day Jesus meets a woman at a well. And this woman has been looking for the perfect husband for years. Jesus knows that:

> The fact is, you have had five husbands, and the man you
> now have is not your husband.   (John 4 v 18)

That's probably why she's at this well in the middle of the day, and on her own. Her "immoral" lifestyle has left her isolated and excluded by others in her town. She has broken all the rules in her pursuit of happiness, but the happiness and fulfilment she longs for remain elusive.

Jesus, though, doesn't ignore her. He doesn't look down on her, or condemn her; he talks to her. He talks to her not because he doesn't know what she's like, but because he does. He knows that she has had five husbands, five failed marriages, five rounds of disappointment, five rounds of hopes dashed and probably five rounds of humiliation to go with it.

And after five husbands, she is still giving it another go, still seeking to find what she is so desperate to find with this sixth man. She is still hoping what most single women hope, even though five sets of failure suggest that she is wrong—that her deepest dreams can be fulfilled in a man.

Jesus understands her heart's deep longing, her deep thirst. And he knows that she's wrong, and right. Wrong, in that no man in her town will truly satisfy her heart's longings. Right, in that there is a man who can.

So he offers her a man who is different. Not just another guy for her to pin all her hopes on, but who will at best disappoint her, and at worst abuse her. No, a man who can bear the weight of all her dreams without being crushed by them.

He offers her himself.

And the key to understanding how Jesus can be this man, how he can fulfil where all others would fail, is in his identity. Towards the end of their conversation...

> The woman said, "I know that Messiah" (called Christ) "is coming. When he comes, he will explain everything to us."

Then Jesus declared, "I, the one speaking to you—I am he."

(v 25-26)

This is no ordinary man. This is the Messiah, the Christ, God's promised King, the ruler for whom God's people have been waiting for centuries. God himself, come to rescue his people, love his people, lead his people.

The man at the well was none other than God himself.

Wrong, and right

What was true of this woman is true of us all. No man can ever be our Saviour. No man can ever give us our ultimate sense of significance, identity, security and purpose and the contentment we long for. They're not perfect.

But unlike the men I had initially found to be perfect until I got to know them, the more we get to know Jesus, and the closer we get to him, the better he appears.

If you've ever suspected that if you just had a man, things would sort themselves out... that having a husband to share your life with would make you content... if you've ever thought: "I'd give anything if I could just find a man to love me"—you're both wrong and right.

You're wrong in that no normal man can manage to do that. If that's what you demand from a future husband, you'll ask too much of him, and then he can only disappoint you. But you're right in that there is a man who came to be that for you. He will never disappoint you, and he wants to be your bridegroom.

He's called Jesus. As we look for what we need, he says to us: "I am he".

That's the theory, anyway. But that's very often not at all what my heart thinks. You may well be reading this thinking: *Yes, I know all that in my head. I know that that's what I'm supposed to think, that Jesus is enough, that he is sufficient, that I can be content in him. But that's certainly not how I feel and that is not my experience. It just doesn't work out in reality. To be honest, I've got Jesus, and I've discovered that my heart longs for someone else, for something more.*

Which is exactly what Israel found. It turned out that God wasn't the husband their hearts desired at all.

3. Deceived

Have you ever watched a married woman grow cold towards her husband? Ever seen a woman who was so in love on her wedding day become hard, critical and bitter about the man she married? Ever seen such a woman eventually leave a good, kind man—the man she had once so loved?

And have you ever seen those things happening and wanted to shout: "You fool! You don't know what you've got and now you're throwing it away!"

In Jeremiah 2, we saw that beautiful picture of the relationship between God, the perfect husband, and Israel, the delighted, devoted bride. But as we return to that passage now, we see that, over time, something extraordinary happened.

We are going to be left with that same feeling: "You fools!" And then we're going to see the challenging, confrontational, unavoidable truth: that we are fools, too.

Drifting apart

Here's what God says to Israel:

> What fault did your ancestors find in me, that they strayed
> so far from me? They followed worthless idols and became
> worthless themselves. They did not ask, "Where is the LORD,
> who brought us up out of Egypt."   (Jeremiah 2 v 5-6)

The devoted bride, who had at one time delighted in her husband, has now strayed far from him. She has wandered off course gradually, little by little, day by day, one step at a time, until she is miles away.

Couples who are splitting up often say things like: "We just drifted apart". There wasn't one big devastating, deciding moment in their relationship that tore them apart. The gulf between them has been the result of hundreds, thousands, of small things that were said or done, and not said or not done; little gestures made, looks given, a word of anger, a tone of voice.

Usually, when a relationship fails there is some fault on both sides, to a greater or lesser degree. But in this relationship between God and his people, he has remained entirely the same as he has always been. It's why he asks: "What fault did your ancestors find in me?"

It is a brave husband who says to his wife: "What did I do wrong?" But God can ask this question of his bride with confidence. There's no fault in him. He hasn't been uncaring, forgetful, or thoughtless. So what's gone wrong?

Israel has fallen in love with someone else. Israel has found someone else who promised more than she feels God is delivering. Her heart has, bit by bit, turned away from him to something else that has so captivated her that there is no room left for her husband.

The idol issue

God calls that something else "idols".

An idol is simply something or someone we love in our hearts as the place where we will find our identity, security and satisfaction. My idol is the thing that I'm chasing, or clinging onto, which is what I think I most need, and which I can't imagine living without.

In Israel's time, it was a carved image or statue. That's probably not particularly attractive to you or me. But an idol can be anything. It could be being married, having children, looking good, being the "right" weight, or having others think well of me. Those are just a few things that have been idols for me over the years.

Idols aren't always bad things. They're more often good things that we make into our god, that we put in God's place in our hearts and therefore in our lives. Why? Because if we have that thing, or more of that thing, then it'll satisfy our heart's deepest longings—won't it? That's what it's promising.

All of us struggle with the pull of worshipping idols. I find it helpful—essential, in fact—to identify what they are for me at the moment. You can't struggle against something you haven't noticed. So it's worth asking yourself: what are the three or four things I'm in most danger of thinking will satisfy my heart's desires?

God's bluntness with Israel about her idols underlines how important it is for us to identify ours. God doesn't call his bride's alternative lovers simply "idols", but "worthless idols". He says they can't, won't, and don't deliver. They offer worth, but they are worthless, and they make their worshippers worthless, too. Israel's worth was in the fact that she was "his", that she was loved by God. But she swapped what was of infinite value for something worthless.

Where to find water

With powerful, vivid imagery, we're given a devastating summary of what Israel has done:

> My people have committed two sins: They have forsaken me,
> the spring of living water, and have dug their own cisterns,
> broken cisterns that cannot hold water. (v 13)

What words come to mind when you think of a "spring of living water"? Fresh? Cool? Clear? Clean? Refreshing? Reviving? Thirst-quenching? Life-giving? And this is a *spring* of water. It just keeps on coming, and never runs dry. This is living water in plentiful, abundant supply.

That spring of living water has a name: God. Israel had a husband who met their deepest needs and satisfied their souls' deepest longings. Yet they turned their backs on all that to dig their own cisterns.

And the problem with their self-built cisterns was that they didn't do what was needed. A cistern was meant to hold fresh, clean water to provide what was needed each day. But their cisterns were broken and leaky. They may have looked like the real thing—but when you needed them, they were useless. They couldn't hold water, and without water you die.

Israel had swapped life for death. God for idols. Water for drought. Like watching a woman who has a great husband growing cold towards him, finding fault with him, and eventually leaving him, we're left wanting to shout: "You fools! Why would you do that?"

It's a good question. Why did Israel turn their backs on the greatest relationship they could have?

Because to them, it looked, and felt, like the obvious thing to do. In their hearts, deep down inside, God did not seem to be meeting their longings. And other things promised to do so.

So either the problem was with God, or the problem was

with their hearts. The problem was with God's word, or with their feelings. Israel, like most of us, followed their hearts. But...

> The heart is deceitful above all things and beyond cure. Who can understand it? (Jeremiah 17 v 9)

What's wrong with following your heart? Nothing—if our hearts always get it right. But they don't. In fact, our hearts deceive us a lot of the time. That's what had happened to Israel. Their own hearts told them to run from the person their own hearts most desired. That's what it means to be self-deceived.

How deceit works

Deceit is all about making something not good look good, or making something good look not good. And being deceived is easier to spot when it's happening to other people than to ourselves (because, by nature, deceit is deceitful!). Being deceived is dangerous because it's so subtle; we're not even aware it's happening.

For deceit to work, good bait is needed. Different bait works in different situations, and different bait works for different prey. I'm no expert on fishing (I tend to think that fish come from a supermarket fridge)—but when it comes to catching some kinds of fish, I vaguely understand that the bait needed is a worm, which is placed on the hook, so that the fish senses the worm, doesn't see the hook, and by the time they do it's too late—they've been hooked.

When it comes to children, worms don't work (for most children, anyway). But there is a classic illustration of deceit in the timeless film *Chitty Chitty Bang Bang*. The child catcher lures the children, Jeremy and Jemima, out of their hiding place and into his trap with his amazing, free lollipops. He shouts up and down the street announcing that his wagon is full of wonderful treats, sweets and chocolate, which are all free. But as soon as the children set foot in the wagon, all the trappings and the façade fall away, and reality is revealed. They realise, too late, that they have been tricked, deceived. They are trapped in a prison containing no lollipops, and from which they cannot escape.

Deceit shows us the bait, dazzles us with the bait, so that we don't see, don't even think about, the hook. The bait fills our vision, captivates our senses, and captures our hearts. We're being offered something that is too good to miss; there's no catch; and we need to grab it now or we might miss our chance (the child catcher knew what he was doing when he announced that his lollipops were "just for today").

Deceit lures us to bite. And we're caught. And the best deceit is the one which so completely lures us that we don't even realise we've been hooked.

How our hearts deceive us

That's what had happened to Israel. They were lured and hooked, deceived by their hearts into loving idols in place of God. And they hadn't even realised that the idol-cisterns were broken.

God isn't only talking about Israel's hearts, though. He's talking about humanity's hearts—our hearts. "The heart is deceitful above all things" (Jeremiah 17 v 9). My heart will tell me that I need to run from the person my own heart most desires.

How does your heart deceive you? What does it tell you? That trusting in yourself, depending on your own strength, and taking matters into your own hands, is better than depending on and trusting in the Lord. It tells you that you need more than God instead of more of God. It deceives you as it convinces you to listen to what the world says, to how you feel, to your own wisdom; as it takes your eyes away from God and fixes them on your circumstances.

Behind the deceit

As we do that, the devil takes advantage and lies to our hearts. He's the one reeling us in, using the deceitful bait.

This has always been his strategy. Back in Genesis 3, in God's very good world, where the first man and woman enjoyed a perfect human marriage and a perfect relationship with their Creator, those first humans decided to reject God's goodness, ignore his words, and destroy their relationship with him and with each other. They chose to eat from the tree that God had commanded them not to.

Why? Because, as the woman realised once it was too late:

The snake deceived me, and I ate.   (Genesis 3 v 13)

The serpent—the devil—had lied to her. He lied in ways he knew would attract her, draw her in, and make her heart say: "Yes, that's right". The devil couldn't make her act. Her heart chose to respond to the temptation as she listened to him. And she chose to follow her heart, to make judgements based on how she felt about what he said.

The devil distracted her from focusing on all that the Lord had given her, all the blessings he had so wonderfully lavished on her and her husband, and from focusing on God himself and the perfect relationship she enjoyed with him. Instead, she listened to the serpent's lies, focused on what the Lord had not given them... and her heart concluded that God was not good, that he was withholding something good from her.

The devil lied, her heart deceived her, and she turned her back on God, on perfection, and on life.

Same old lies

The two lies the devil used then have proved very successful ever since. The first lie is that God is not good. The devil suggested to the woman that God had restricted her from eating from that one tree not because he knew what was best for her, but because he wanted to hold back what was best for her.

The devil whispers to our hearts: *Look at your situation. God isn't really being good to you, is he? He's withholding something good from you, something that you need. Can he really love you if he's doing that?*

The second lie is that God's word is not true. The devil asks the woman: "Did God really say...?" When she confirms that God had warned that eating from that one tree would result in death, he argues: "You will not certainly die".

So the devil whispers to our hearts: *God doesn't really know what he's talking about. You can't really believe what he says.*

His tactics are always the same—to get us to doubt God's goodness and doubt God's word. As he does that, he whispers to our hearts the three words that we most fear: *You're missing out.*

We're listening to this message all the time, from within and without. Israel was then, and we are now. Our hearts are no different from Adam's and Eve's, and no different from Israel's. And the devil has not changed, either.

Spotting the bait

It's easy for us to see so clearly past the bait to the hooks when it comes to fish and children. Even as a child, whenever I watched *Chitty Chitty Bang Bang*, I shouted at the screen to Jeremy and Jemima: "Stay in your hiding place! You fools!" It was so obviously a trap!

But we're not fish and we're not children, so we wouldn't fall for those things, would we?

Israel sought relationships with and fulfilment from statues— why? Because that's what the nations around her did. As the devil showed Eve the fruit that was nearby, within reach, and looked so good, and her heart deceived her, so Israel looked at the nations that were nearby, and so powerful and their hearts deceived them. They didn't want to miss out.

So what will it be for us? For you? You live in a culture in which sex is everywhere, and sex seems to equal fulfilment. That's the whisper your heart hears every day, and if you're a single, celibate woman, the bait is: *You're not having sex. You're missing out on what you most need.*

If you go to church, you are part of a community which probably puts great emphasis on marriage; and so a husband to serve Christ with and spend life with, and children to love and bring up, seems to equal fulfilment. That's the whisper your heart hears every Sunday: *You're not married, you're not a mother. You're missing out on what you most need.*

So when it comes to the single woman, what is one of the fruits, statues, baits most likely to be successful in luring her in? A husband.

4. How to run from God

Two significant things happened to me when I was 22. The first was that I became a Christian. The second was that, at last, I started dating a guy I had been in love with for 3 years... who wasn't a Christian.

Joel was funny; he was handsome; he made me go weak at the knees (literally—I once walked into a room, saw him, and had to lean up against a wall because my legs were giving way!) Because I loved Joel, I started going out with him. Because I had become a Christian, I started going to church and joined a Bible-study group. I loved both Joel and my new church.

Which man?

But there was a problem. As we studied the Bible each week, I came to see that if Jesus was the Lord of my life, my relationship with him was the most important thing in my life. That meant that all my decisions—including who I should marry—needed to be ones which helped me to grow in that relationship.

And that led me to the unwelcome (at that time) but inescapable conclusion that someone who didn't know Jesus, and didn't want to know Jesus, couldn't be the man I should, or could, marry. And Joel didn't know Jesus.

But Joel meant everything to me and, as I think I mentioned, he was gorgeous! Here's how my internal thinking went: *But I love him. I really do. So surely it's OK? I'm not marrying him anyway, I'm just going out with him. And so that can't be wrong. I love him.**

One day, after I'd been in the Bible-study group for a few months, the leader invited me round for tea. She was an older lady, who we all respected but were also just a little bit scared of. She poured me a cup of tea, passed me a piece of cake, chatted for a bit and then came out with: "Now my dear, about the boyfriend" (she really did say those exact words!).

Then she proceeded, gently and lovingly, to point out that my relationship with Joel was not good, and was not godly. She showed me verses in the Bible, and we talked about what they meant. She pointed me to Jesus. As she spoke I sipped my tea, ate my cake, and nodded... And inside, I was absolutely furious.

How dare she? Who was she to tell me what to do? She didn't know how much I loved Joel, how happy he made me, how my heart skipped a beat when I thought about him. I sat there, smiling externally and seething internally.

Making a choice

When it was finally over, I went home and reflected on what she had said. I thought about why I was so angry, and realised that it

---

* If you want to think more about what the Bible says about a Christian marrying a non-Christian, go to page 85.

was because I knew that everything she had said was right and was true. I just didn't want to hear it.

I didn't want to give up this man. He made me happy. He made me laugh. He made me feel secure. He made me feel wanted and loved. He was the subject of my daydreams. I was his girlfriend... and maybe one day I would be his wife.

Slowly, it dawned on me that life had become about him. My identity, security and contentment were all wrapped up in my relationship with him. If push came to shove, I'd rather lose Jesus than lose him. He had, I suddenly realised, become an idol.

I knew that ending my relationship with Joel was the right thing to do, but I couldn't imagine that I'd actually be able to do it. I felt extremely weak, unsure and frightened. I asked the Lord to help me do what my heart didn't really want to do. And God was very kind: as I ended things with Joel, I was aware of God's strength and peace in the midst of the very real pain. And he surrounded me with Christian friends who loved me, prayed for me and helped me to find in Jesus what I'd been looking for in Joel.

At the time, it felt as though I was giving up the world, everything I needed. But looking back, what I had wanted for myself was far too small. Jesus wanted me to be more fulfilled, satisfied, content and joyful than I wanted me to be. I would have settled for Joel, and though he was a great guy, he was not a perfect guy. I would have settled for Joel, and given up on Jesus. And Jesus wanted more for me than that.

My next mistake

I learned a lot from that experience. I learned that the Christian life is not easy. I learned that Jesus deserved to be my priority.

And I learned that I needed a Christian husband. So I spent the rest of my twenties and into my thirties looking for him.

He never arrived. And it has been good for me to look back as a 42-year-old, as I've written this book, and ask myself the question: *Why did I want a Christian husband?*

As I've looked into my heart, I've seen an answer that I like. I wanted a Christian husband so that I could have someone who I could be close to and intimate with, and who I could serve the Lord with. I wanted someone who I could encourage and support in ministry. We would help each other grow in godliness as we prayed together, served together, were hospitable together. I longed to bring honour and glory to Jesus... with a husband. Those good desires were in my heart.

But as I've looked further into my heart, I've seen that there was another, deeper answer, one that I really don't like. When I thought about my ideal husband, I had a bit of a recurring daydream; and the content of my daydream gave away the real desires of my heart.

I used to daydream about being married to an amazingly gifted, well-known Bible teacher—not a specific one, an imaginary one. In my daydream, people would frequently come up to me and say things like: "Oh wow, are you married to him? Isn't your husband amazing?! He's so gifted and godly and humble and funny!" (In the daydream, he was also good-looking, and everyone else noticed that too but, being Christians, they just thought it and didn't say it.) And I would think: "Yes, that's my husband".

In my daydream, my focus wasn't on the fact that my husband was being used by God, and that God was being honoured and glorified through him. My focus was on the fact that I was being honoured and glorified for having such a great husband, for being the kind of woman who would be married to such a godly man.

I was making the same mistake as I did with Joel. I was wanting a husband in whom to find my identity, my satisfaction and my value. I was still making a husband into an idol. Not that it was wrong to want a husband—but that it was wrong to want a husband for those reasons. I still needed to learn to find those things in Jesus. And I'm still learning!

Where the husband-idol leads us

Analysing that daydream about the Christian husband I never found has been really helpful to me. It's easy to see how making an idol out of Joel could have led me to leave church and turn my back on Jesus. But it's possible to make an idol out of having a Christian husband, and when he never comes along, stay in church and turn my back on Jesus.

How does this look? Where does the husband-idol lead us? The following characters are fictional but based on real life. There are bits of me, at various times in my life, and bits of many other women I have come across in both "Sally" and "Maya". They may describe you partly or completely as you read.

Although it's often unsettling, raw and painful to look properly at our hearts, remember that this is where our struggles begin and are mainly fought. So as you read, try to take a good look at your own heart and see if it is reflected in theirs.

Sally

Sally had waited for years. She had prayed: "Dear Lord, please give me a Christian husband". She had kept praying and waiting, praying and waiting, but still she had no husband. All her friends seemed to have met and married someone, but it had never happened to her.

People at church had kept encouraging her. They had said that the Lord would have someone "special" for her; that she should keep praying and making sure she would make a good wife, and that they were sure someone would come along soon.

Sally read her Bible, and tried to find verses that would help her. Her particular favourite became:

Delight yourself in the LORD and he will give you the desires
of your heart.   (Psalm 37 v 4, NIV84)

She knew what the desires of her heart were. There was really only one desire: to be married. So she set about trying very hard to delight herself in the Lord.

She "delighted" herself in the Lord by regularly leading a children's group at church, cooking for some elderly neighbours, helping at the kids summer holiday club, hosting her Bible-study group, and reading her Bible and praying each day. She was doing a lot more delighting than most other Christians she knew.

But no husband came. Time passed, and having a husband became more and more important to her. And, though Sally wasn't aware of it happening, her heart began to believe that God was not good. The more she "delighted" herself in the Lord, the more bitter she became.

Although Sally kept it all inside, she was angry at God. He hadn't kept his side of the bargain. She had "delighted" herself in the Lord and he had not given her the desires of her heart. She had been a good girl for years, and now she deserved her husband; she had earned her husband! The devil had been whispering those lies that he loves to tell: *God is not good, he has*

not given you what your heart desires. God's word is not true, he has
not given you what he said he would.

This was clearly true. God hadn't done what he'd promised. Her life became full of resentment and discontentment. Her constant thought, as she looked around and compared herself to others, was: "It's not fair! Why has she got a husband and I haven't?"

Sally has continued to go to church. She still does her "duty" and goes through the motions; she's a really committed church member. But she has no joy inside, and no love to give. Her heart is full of envy and self-pity. God has let her down. Sally is single, she doesn't have a husband, and she doesn't know a good God. She doesn't love him anymore. Why should she?

Maya

Maya's experience had been similar to Sally's, but after a few years of delighting herself in the Lord and waiting for her Christian husband, she began to feel more and more that she didn't "fit in" at church as a single person. Though at first she pushed the idea away, she began to wonder if life lived the Bible's way didn't really work. Did God really want her to feel like this—out of place, and unfulfilled?

Then Maya met Tom. He was friendly and thoughtful, and she found that she didn't feel lonely when she was talking with him. He wasn't a Christian, but he was a lot more interested in and attentive to her than any of the single men at church had ever been.

When he asked her out, Maya knew she should say no. But she also knew she needed to say yes. No one else had asked her out for years. It was only a date. And Tom made her feel happy. Deep down, she was thrilled he wanted to be more than friends.

Surely Jesus would want her to be happy? She made clear to Tom that her faith meant she wouldn't sleep with him outside of marriage, and would be going to church on Sunday mornings. He said he respected that; so Maya went on the first date. And a second, and third. Soon, Tom and Maya were an item.

Not long after, what had once been "too far" felt "so good". Maya had never felt happier. Tom was the perfect man for her. She felt a bit bad that she was leaving Tom's bed, instead of her own, to go to church on a Sunday morning. But more than that, she felt that the people at church didn't understand her. When one of her church friends challenged her about Tom, it was clear that something had to change. Maya stopped going to church. She had found the life she wanted; she had found the man she needed.

Last week, Maya bumped into someone from her old Bible-study group. She told them how happy she is. She's moved in with Tom, and they're very much in love. He's not a Christian, but then, she says, that doesn't really matter—because neither is she.

Delighting in…

Sally and Maya had both, genuinely, been thinking they were "delighting themselves in the Lord". But their hearts had deceived them. They were in fact delighting themselves in themselves; and so, when they didn't get what they wanted—what they thought they needed—they rejected God.

They did it in different ways, though. One did it by leaving, and the other did it by staying. One doesn't come to church anymore—the other is there every week.

Maya and Sally are like the two brothers in a story Jesus told about two brothers who lived with their father (who represents God).

The younger one said to his father: "Father, give me my share
of the estate." So he divided his property between them. Not
long after that, the younger son got together all he had, set
off for a distant country and there squandered his wealth in
wild living. After he had spent everything, there was a severe
famine in that whole country, and he began to be in need.

(Luke 15 v 12-14)

In asking for his share of the inheritance, the younger brother
is effectively saying that he wishes that his father was dead. His
father, amazingly, does what he wants, and the younger brother
leaves home, heading for a far-off country. He wastes the money
in reckless living and ends up in a pigsty, lonely, hungry and
friendless.

Maya has made the same decision. She has decided that life is
better lived her way than God's; better lived without God than with
him. There are a whole number of ways people do this; it happens
whenever someone, whether guy or girl, single or married, decides
that life is better lived without God than with him.

In Maya's case, she walked away from God to be with Tom.
And sadly, sooner or later Tom will disappoint her, will let her
down, will prove to be less than she dreamed of. Of course he
will—he's just a guy! The life far away from God glitters, but it
deceives.

In the story, the younger brother:

came to his senses [and] said ... "Here I am starving to death!
I will set out and go back to my father'. (v 17-18)

He admitted his mistake, and returned to find that he could be
forgiven and welcomed back by the only one he'd really needed:
his father. Sadly, most "Mayas" don't come back. They live with
less than they could have enjoyed; they die without the only
relationship that matters beyond death.

It is obvious to see how this younger son has rejected his father, but what about the other one?

The older brother has stayed at home; he has been a good son. Until, that is, the younger brother returns home, and their father is filled with compassion, runs to meet his son, welcomes him home, and calls for a huge party. What would happen when the older brother found out?

> [He] became angry and refused to go in ... [he said to] his father, "Look! All these years I've been slaving for you and never disobeyed your orders. Yet you never gave me even a young goat so I could celebrate with my friends. But when this son of yours who has squandered your property with prostitutes comes home, you kill the fattened calf for him!"
>
> (v 28-30)

This is Sally. She hasn't run away like Maya. She's done the right thing. And now she looks at married women in church who aren't as "good" as her, and she becomes angry. She's slaved for God for years, and they get a husband while she gets nothing. How is that fair?

Although what they do looks very different on the surface, the heart issue for both brothers is the same. Both wanted what the father could give them, not the father himself.

Which is exactly what Jesus' listeners were doing when it came to God. Jesus told the story to:

> tax collectors and sinners [who] were all gathering round to hear Jesus [and to] the Pharisees and the teachers of the law [who] muttered, "This man welcomes sinners, and eats with them." (v 1-2)

Jesus told it to make the point that you can just as easily reject God by "staying" and doing your duty, by being moral and trying to be good (like the Pharisees and teachers of the law), as you can by "going" and being reckless and obviously disobedient (like the tax collectors and "sinners"). You can just as easily, though less noticeably, reject God by becoming Sally as becoming Maya.

Sally, Maya… and you

Of course, we don't all fit neatly into one of those two categories, although my guess is that all of our hearts will tend to be more susceptible to being like the younger or older brother at different times of life, or in different areas of life. I can be getting on with disobeying God in one area of my life, while looking down on others for disobeying in a different area where I am "better".

But it's worth pausing to take time to ask ourselves some questions which help us to see ways in which our hearts are, or are in danger of being, like Sally's and/or Maya's:

1. What do you daydream about?

2. What do you pray for?

   Do you bother to pray at all, since God hasn't given you what you asked for (or has taken away what you once had, if you are widowed or divorced or used to be in a sexual relationship)?

   Do you ask for God's glory first, as the Lord's Prayer teaches, or do you just pray for a husband?

3. What motivates what you do "for the Lord"?

4. Why do you want a husband? It's not wrong to want to be married—but it's good to be honest with ourselves about why we want to be married.

5. If you're honest, do you think that having a husband who isn't a Christian is better than not having a husband at all? If so, why?

6. Are you, right now, feeling like Maya did? Or like Sally did? Are you walking down, or have you walked all the way down, one of their paths?

5. Why to run to God

If you're reading this book and have got this far, the chances are that you're reasonably convinced that you don't want to end up like the younger brother in the middle of Jesus' parable; or like the older brother at the end of it—outside the father's house, out of relationship with him, and missing out on the party. In other words, you don't want to be Maya, settling for second best, for the slow-dawning realisation that rejecting God wasn't a fulfilling or satisfying decision; or Sally, increasing in bitterness, falling out of love with a God who seems so disappointing.

So when you struggle with singleness—when your heart tells you that what you most need is very simply not to be single anymore—how can you avoid becoming Maya or Sally?

There are two ways to seek to avoid it. And only one of those works.

A fable lesson

Aesop's fables are only really ever read by children. And they're wasted on children! Here's one I love:

"The Wind and the Sun were disputing which was the stronger. Suddenly, they saw a traveller coming down the road, and the

Sun said: 'I see a way to decide our dispute. Whichever of us can cause that traveller to take off his cloak shall be regarded as the stronger. You begin.' So the Sun retired behind a cloud, and the Wind began to blow as hard as he could upon the traveller. But the harder he blew, the more closely did the traveller wrap his cloak round him, till at last the Wind had to give up in despair. Then the Sun came out and shone in all his glory upon the traveller, who soon found he had no need to keep his cloak on."

This is a great description of the two ways we can try, when we feel burdened by the weight of our singleness, to deal with that burden without rejecting God. It is a description of the difference between religion and the gospel.

Religion makes us try to be better at being good and godly. If we can only think and act correctly, if we can make enough of an effort, then we will stop disliking our singleness, we'll start seeing it as a gift, and we'll get it "right". When we fail to think or feel like that, we need to try harder to be better; to become more and more religious.

The gospel, on the other hand, warms and melts our hearts, and changes us from the inside out. We do the right thing not because we have to or ought to, but because it is the natural thing to do, the thing we want to do.

Religion, ultimately, leads to covering up or giving up, because it doesn't work. The gospel allows us to be ourselves and enjoy being Christians, because it makes a real difference.

How to take your cloak off

If the "cloak" in the fable represents feeling the weight of singleness, the question to ask is: How can I take it off?

Here's the religious approach. We read 1 Corinthians 7 and remind ourselves that singleness is a gift from God that we can, and should, accept and be thankful for. We remember all the blessings and advantages of being single. We just try to stop thinking about it. We seek to replace negative feelings with positive ones; we throw ourselves into church life; we pray. We put a lot of effort into being godly about our singleness. Like the wind, we blow very, very hard. And none of these things are wrong, or bad. But of themselves, they won't help. They won't make a difference.

Although it's not in the original book, there is a great line in the BBC adaptation of *Pride and Prejudice* at the stage where Darcy has been rejected by Lizzie, and is trying to get over his love for her. He goes fencing, throws himself into it, and mutters to himself: "I shall conquer this. I shall." That's "religion"—trying by force of will and a bit of distraction to get things "right", and convince yourself that you don't feel a certain way.

Capturing our own hearts

If we are in that situation, where religious effort or self-persuasion is our motivation and method, or if we are in the same mindset as Sally or Maya—what we need is for our heart to be captured by something bigger and better than the issue of having or not having a husband for this life; something much bigger and better.

Our hearts are all thirsty, desperately thirsty. They were made to be quenched, but, like the woman who met Jesus in John 4, we naturally look in all the wrong places to quench that thirst.

Let's go back to the well and just listen to what Jesus says to her.

> Everyone who drinks this water will be thirsty again, but
> whoever drinks the water I give them will never thirst.
> Indeed, the water I give them will become in them a spring
> of water welling up to eternal life.   (John 4 v 13-14)

No other "water" satisfies the thirst. All the other places, things and relationships we may look to ultimately leave us wanting something more, or something different. This includes marriage. It's very easy to forget that all married people would like it to be better, and some married people would like to be married to someone other than their spouse. Marriage does include "many troubles" (1 Corinthians 7 v 28). Ask an honest, married Christian, and they'll tell you that marriage cannot bear the weight of having all our hopes, dreams and longings placed upon it.

Jesus can. Jesus says: *Taste my water, and you'll never thirst again.* As he puts it a few chapters later in John:

> "Let anyone who is thirsty come to me and drink. Whoever
> believes in me, as Scripture has said, rivers of living water
> will flow from within them." By this he meant the Spirit.
>
>   (7 v 37-39)

Dying of thirst

Jesus knows that everyone is thirsty. But not everyone knows that they are, and you've got to know you're thirsty in order to come and drink.

Imagine seeing someone die of thirst right next to a vast, limitless ocean of fresh, cool drinking water that was theirs for the taking... because they didn't think they were thirsty. It would be madness; yet it's so easy for us to listen to Jesus' invitation and not realise that we are spiritually thirsty, desperately thirsty—that in fact, without him, we are dying of thirst.

To "drink" is to "believe", to put my trust in Jesus Christ instead of all the other possibilities: my looks, wardrobe, intellect, achievements, job, relationship, children, home, friendships, what people think of me—anything that I can achieve or earn myself.

Jesus' living water transforms us as his Holy Spirit enables us to see how beautiful, precious and infinitely worthy Jesus is. We need to see how he has loved us, and what he has done to make us his own, so that our hearts will be captivated by him.

That's all very well—but why should you allow your heart to be full of Jesus, rather than something or someone else. Why should Maya choose Jesus over Tom? I have heard lots of single women say to me over the years: "But how do I really know Jesus loves me?" or "How do I really know that Jesus will do what's best for me?"

We can know he loves us, not just because he says he does, but because of what he has done for us. The answer to those questions is easy to say, though hard to apply: the gospel.

Holding out a cup

Have you ever read one of the accounts of Jesus's death? If you haven't, why not look up Mark 14 – 16?

If you have read it often, it's still worth reading again. But it's also worth remembering that familiarity can breed complacency. We can easily read the words without really being impacted by the events they describe. I know this because I do it.

So let's pause to remember the fact that although fully God, Jesus was also fully man. He had real emotions, he felt real feelings. He experienced joy and compassion and sorrow and tiredness and pain, just as we do. He had real choices, like any man.

In the garden of Gethsemane, late on a Thursday night, we see the rawness of his agony and distress as he tells his disciples that his soul is "overwhelmed to the point of death" (Mark 14 v 34). From the depths of this pain, he cries out to his Father:

> Everything is possible for you. Take this cup from me.
>
> (14 v 36)

As he knelt in that garden, Jesus knew he would die the next day; and he knew that what lay ahead was not just an unimaginably painful physical death, horrific as that would be. No, the main cause of his anguish was this "cup" that he was going to drink. In the Old Testament, when God warned that his enemies would be judged and punished, he used the image of them drinking from a cup which would make them "stagger" (Jeremiah 25 v 15-16; see also Psalm 75 v 7-8). That is what Jesus was facing, why he was emotionally staggering. God's wrath, God's righteous anger, was being poured into that cup. Jesus, God's perfect, spotless, sinless Son, was facing the prospect of drinking it down to the very last bitter dregs.

Why?

Two questions should spring to our minds. Why was the Father holding this cup out to his Son? And why would his Son drink it?

The Father was holding it out to his Son so that he doesn't hold it out to us. Here's how he explained what would happen, hundreds of years before (the plan was so certain that it's written about as though it had already happened):

> He was pierced for our transgressions,
>   he was crushed for our iniquities;
> the punishment that brought us peace was upon him,
>   and by his wounds we are healed.
> We all, like sheep have gone astray,
>   each of us has turned to his own way;
>   and the Lord has laid on him
>   the iniquity of us all.   (Isaiah 53 v 5-6)

The cup was held out to Jesus on the cross so that it doesn't need to be held out to you and me when we die, and then held out to us for ever beyond our deaths. By his wounds we would be healed. Jesus would stand in our place and take the eternal punishment which we deserve. He would stand in our place and feel the shame and disgrace of the ways we have rejected God, hurt others, and abused his world; he would bear the judgment on all the wrong things we have all thought said and done... as if he himself had thought, said and done those things.

That was why God the Father held out the cup to his Son.

But would Jesus, this sinless man who didn't deserve a drop of that cup, drink it?

Taking the cup

Surely not. In the garden, he was overwhelmed just by its prospect. He began to taste the horror of experiencing our punishment. He cried out for the cup to be taken away from him. And then he prayed what I think is one of the most amazing sentences in the Bible:

> Yet not what I will, but what you will.   (Mark 14 v 36)

He took the cup. He was arrested, mocked, humiliated, tortured and crucified.

> And when they had mocked him, they took off the purple robe and put his own clothes on him. Then they led him out to crucify him. (Mark 15 v 20)

Jesus could have stopped what was happening at any time. He had armies of angels at his disposal. Yet he did nothing. Christ chose to take the cup, to die on the cross, to bear his Father's wrath and to experience the awfulness, for the first time in eternity, of having to shout:

> My God, my God, why have you forsaken me? (v 34)

He chose to die.

> With a loud cry, Jesus breathed his last. The curtain of the temple was torn in two from top to bottom. (v 37-38)

The thick, heavy temple curtain hung between the main part of the temple and the Most Holy Place at the heart of the temple, where God's presence dwelt. Only one man—the high priest— was allowed in there, just once a year, and even then only after going through a long process of ritual purification. The curtain was like a "No Entry" sign, making clear that imperfect people could not come into the presence of a perfect God. The judgment of God stood between people and the relationship with God that they were designed to enjoy, that they were made to long for.

That's why the curtain tore. Jesus had taken that judgment. He had drunk the cup. He had stood where we should stand, and taken the punishment we should face. If we trust in what Jesus has done—if we trust he did it for *us*—we are now able to come into God's presence and enjoy relationship with him. We can now receive Jesus' perfection, so that when the Father looks at you and me, he sees a perfect bride.

We contributed nothing but our sin. He did it all for us... he did it all for me.

Only love would do this. Only the most loving, caring, compassionate, unselfish man would choose to go through all that for you. Only the most amazing person would know what you most needed before you did, would understand the cost of giving it to you, and then come and live and die in order to offer you what your heart truly needs.

Does Jesus love you? The gospel message says: *Look at the cross*. Does Jesus truly know what's best for you? The gospel says: *Look at the cross*.

You may have read this story hundreds of times before. You may have it word for word in your head, it's so familiar. You may have skipped bits as you read because you know it. Or maybe it's all new to you—you've never before heard it put this way or realised why Jesus died. But whether it's old or new to you, the question is: How do those truths make you *feel*?

Overwhelmed

I can clearly remember being overwhelmed once on holiday when I was about ten, as a massive wave came in while I was knee-deep in the sea. As I watched it getting nearer, I thought I would be able to stand my ground, but it was so huge and mighty and powerful that it knocked me completely off my feet. It totally overwhelmed me.

Jesus was overwhelmed with sorrow in the garden of Gethsemane. Why? So that we can be overwhelmed with something very different.

What happens when we come to Jesus, with an open humble heart, and "drink"? His Spirit comes into our hearts, to make

Jesus more and more real, and more and more precious to us. He enables us to grasp more of who Jesus is, and what he's like, and what he's done, and what he's doing, and what he's going to do. As that happens, we will be overwhelmed by his great love for us. We will look at the cross, and we will be knocked off our feet.

The cross tells me that God loves me. It puts it beyond all doubt. If that truth has even slightly impacted my heart, can I really begin to imagine that, because he hasn't given me a husband, he doesn't love me? Am I really going to believe that he died for me, took God's judgment for me, and gave eternal life to me, but doesn't love me because marriage isn't (at least for the moment) a part of his plan for getting me from here to heaven? Am I *really* going to make the measure of his love whether he gives me a husband, instead of whether he gave his life for me?

This is the gospel. It overwhelms us with the love of this man.

When we even just begin to appreciate God's love for us in Jesus, he becomes more precious than anything else to us. Our outward circumstances matter less and less, because he means so much more. We are satisfied if we have him. This is what the early Christian leader Paul called the "secret" of contentment:

> I have learned to be content whatever the circumstances. I know what it is to be in need, and I know what it is to have plenty. I have learned the secret of being content in any and every situation, whether well fed or hungry, whether living in plenty or in want. I can do all this through him who gives me strength. (Philippians 4 v 11-13)

Paul was in prison, facing death. But he had taken hold of a contentment that had nothing to do with outward circumstances, and everything to do with an eternal relationship.

Back to the fable

To return to Aesop: *The Sun is the Son!*

If you feel that you live under the burden of "being single", if it has come to define you and dominate you, the answer is not to try and take it off, try to leave it off, try to leave it behind. The answer is to look at Jesus, to enjoy his love, to warm yourself in who you are in him.

Then you'll find yourself not trying to take the cloak off, not grappling to cast it off, but simply removing it to bask in the Son. The way not to be Sally, grudging and bitter and unloving, or Maya, turning her back on Jesus in order to turn her back on singleness, is, in a sense, to do nothing at all; except to look at, dwell on, and love being overwhelmed, time and time again, by what Jesus has done for you.

So, bask in the Son!

6. Singleness: a gift

In pride of place in my bedroom hangs a painting which a friend painted for my 30th birthday of Cannizaro Park in Wimbledon Village, southwest London. It's a beautiful park, and it's very special to me. Over the years, I've spent many happy hours there playing with my godsons, walking and talking with friends, lying in the sun and just enjoying some time on my own.

So this painting is very precious—when I look at it, it makes me smile. But the place itself is much more precious to me. I love staring at the painting, but that doesn't even begin to compare with actually being in the park.

That painting is an image of the reality; and the Bible says that human marriage, too, is a picture of a greater reality:

> The husband is the head of the wife as Christ is the head
> of the church, his body, of which he is the Saviour. Now as
> the church submits to Christ, so also wives should submit
> to their husbands in everything. Husbands, love your wives,
> just as Christ loved the church and gave himself up for her to
> make her holy.   (Ephesians 5 v 23-26)

There is loads there about how a Christian marriage is best conducted, but to focus only on human husbands and wives is to miss the big point that God is making here. Marriage is a picture, a precious picture but nevertheless only a picture, of the relationship between Christ and his church—believers.

So if we are part of the church, we are enjoying the amazing, ultimate reality of Jesus being our Husband! Human husbands are a wonderful blessing from God, but the best of them is only a pale reflection of the perfect Husband all believers have. Human husbands may be gracious, godly men, but there is no other husband like Christ our head and Saviour; no other husband who always knows what's best for us, and who is not only willing but able always to do what is best for us.

The picture, human marriage, is very good, but the reality it points to is infinitely better!

Relationship status

This means that single Christians are not incomplete without "the one". In fact, we already have the ultimate One. No, the "relationship status" that defines us and dominates our affections as part of his people is not "single" but "married to Christ". It's as we realise how amazing Jesus is that our hearts begin to see where our true identity lies. We begin to say not: "I'm a single woman (*identity*) who happens to be a Christian (*circumstances*)", but: "I'm a Christian (*identity*) who happens to be single (*circumstances*)".

Way back in the Old Testament (and way back in this book!), we were told that for God's people: "Your Maker is your husband" (Isaiah 54 v 5). In Jesus, and most of all in the death of Jesus, we see beyond all doubt that our Maker is not only our Husband, but he is our loving Husband. He is the One to whom all human husbands point every time they do anything loving, thoughtful, or self-giving. But how easy it is to have the ultimate, yet never enjoy him because we are so focused on not having the picture. It's like me having a flat on the edge of Cannizaro Park, enjoying a panoramic view of the whole park from my window, and yet never looking out of the window because I'm so disappointed that I don't have a 20-by-14-inch painting of the park hanging on my bedroom wall.

That's the perspective that Sally and Maya both had, in different ways. Both wanted more than Jesus, felt they needed more than Jesus. What their hearts really need, and what all our hearts really only ever need, is more of Jesus.

All things work for good(?)

People often tell me that their favourite Bible verse is Romans 8 v 28:

> And we know that in all things God works for the good of those who love him, who have been called according to his purpose.

This is a precious truth that can be a great comfort, but it does pose a question: What is "good"?

When I get to define what "good" means, I come up with something like: "good = what I want". It is what is painless and pleasurable, and it is definitely not what is painful or difficult in any way. If that is my understanding of "good", what happens when I have prayed about something and the Lord has not answered in the way that I wanted? I am left, just like Sally and Maya, thinking: *This is not good* and so I end up defining God through my disappointments. I say to myself: *God has not given me what is good,* even though he promised to in Romans 8 v 28; and so I can only conclude either that "God is not good" or that God does not tell the truth.

But the next verse gives us a very different definition of what is "good"—and it's God's definition:

> For those God foreknew he also predestined to be conformed
> to the image of his Son, that he might be the firstborn among
> many brothers and sisters. (v 29)

"Good" is not giving me whatever circumstances I like; it is God using circumstances to make me like his Son. Everything that happens in our lives, without exception, God somehow uses to make us more like the Lord Jesus. That is the good we can know God is doing, which is very different from "getting what I want". This kind of good may be painful—in fact in some situations it is likely to be very painful—but it is the way that our loving heavenly Father enables us to grow.

As so often in the Bible, we are very quickly pointed to the cross as the place to get our perspective:

> If God is for us, who can be against us? He who did not spare
> his own Son, but gave him up for us all—how will he not
> also, along with him, graciously give us all things?" (v 31-32)

Jesus died for you, so he's hardly going to hold back on giving you other good things now! Jesus never thinks: *I did die for Andrea, but I just can't be bothered to sort her out with a husband, though that would be best* or: *Oh, if only I could find Andrea a husband. It's what she needs but I just can't find the right man!* or: *Oops, I meant to get Andrea married but I forgot. Ah well, she'll just have to stay single now.* Jesus is in control of our circumstances and he is working in our circumstances for our good. Rather than feeling: *It wasn't meant to be like this*, we can be confident that in fact, even when we can't see why or how, it was meant to be *exactly* like this!

The gift of singleness

When God talks about singleness being a gift, we'll only be able to agree with him if we remember who the gift is from. It is from Jesus, who loves us more than we'll ever really grasp, and who would do (and has done) anything and everything we need. We need to remember it's a gift from the perfect Husband, and a good husband does what's best for his wife, not what's easiest or makes her happiest in the short term.

When we know Jesus in this way, we don't love him in order to get the circumstances we want (like a husband); we use our circumstances in order to serve the One we love. We see our circumstances—both the ones we'd have chosen, and the ones we wouldn't—as opportunities not just to grow like Jesus, but to serve Jesus. That's why Paul says:

> I would like you to be free from concern ... An unmarried woman or virgin is concerned about the Lord's affairs: her aim is to be devoted to the Lord in both body and spirit. But a married woman is concerned about the affairs of this world—how she can please her husband. I am saying this for your own good, not to restrict you, but that you may live in a right way in undivided devotion to the Lord.
>
> (1 Corinthians 7 v 32, 34-35)

I'm single; and that means that each moment of my day I can spend in undivided, delighted devotion to Jesus, who loves me so much and so well. I don't need to consider anyone else's interests other than his as I decide where to live, what to do, how to spend my time and what to spend my money on. Singleness is a gift that is making me more like the person I was designed to be, sometimes in ways I can see and sometimes in ways that I can't. And singleness is a gift that, if I can only see it, I can use to serve my Lord. If you are single, you're receiving that gift too.

When we find our relationship status in knowing Jesus, we are able to see that singleness is not a quiet tragedy, but a great opportunity. We can see singleness as a gift—probably not one we chose, but one we have been lovingly given—and therefore a good gift.

True delight

And this means we can really live out Psalm 37 v 4:

> Delight yourself in the Lord, and he will give you the desires of your heart. (NIV84)

Sally's and Maya's way of "delighting themselves in the Lord" focused entirely on themselves. They saw Jesus as a means to an end. Their thinking was: "If I do something for the Lord, then he will give me what I want". Rather than using the opportunity that being single gave them to grow in love for the Lord, they reacted by trying to manipulate him into giving them a husband, or they turned their back on him to get a husband for themselves.

But that's not delighting in the Lord. That's using the Lord while delighting in what you think he will give you. Truly delighting yourself in the Lord focuses on him. It is to:

> Delight yourself *in the Lord*, and he will give you the desires of your heart.

When we ask him to help us see more and more of who he is, what he's done for us and what he wants for our lives, then our hearts see the truth, and stop being deceived; we see that our deepest longings, our greatest desires, are all satisfied in him. Jesus stops being a means to an end, where we attach the provision of a husband as a condition of us loving him; he becomes the ultimate end, our greatest desire, and the only Person we need.

That's who he is for the Christian, married as well as unmarried. It's not that single people delight in Jesus because they can't delight in a spouse. It's that every Christian delights in Jesus, finds in him that they have been given all they ever really wanted, and then uses everything else they have—singleness, marriage, children, career, and so on—to serve him.

Count your blessings

My 93-year-old grandma is a wonderful woman. She's been a Christian since she was a little girl, and still sings hymns in bed as she goes to sleep each night. One of her favourite hymns is an old one called "Count Your Blessings", which I have come to love too. One part of it goes:

Count your blessings, name them one by one,
And it will surprise you what the Lord has done.

My grandma is single, though she hasn't always been. She was married for 29 years, and has been a widow for the last 44. She was, of course, devastated when her husband died, and in great pain as she grieved for him. She missed him terribly. But she was joyful and satisfied even as she grieved, because she had not ultimately been finding her identity, security and hope in her husband. She had found those in her Lord, and he was with her, even in her great loss; and he continues to be with her day by day.

My grandmother would say that being married was good, but that being single is good too, because in both circumstances she has her Lord; and because, as she puts it: "The Lord knows, and he doesn't make mistakes".

Grandma would never have chosen for her husband to die. But she can look back and see how God has used it for good, because she knows "good" is whatever makes her more like Jesus and enables her to serve Jesus.

It didn't have to be like that, though. If she had focused on herself and her loss, if she had dwelt upon how her plans for her life had been taken away, she would have become bitter and twisted, angry with God and envious of those who still had their husbands. She would have spent 44 years hardening her heart and not enjoying Jesus' love or the life he's given her.

But she looked to the Lord, remembered that he loved her, trusted him when it was toughest, and knew that he was in loving charge of every circumstance. And now she radiates Christ-likeness; she is kind and compassionate, and she has a wonderful ability to empathise with and get alongside and say the right thing to people who are struggling or in pain.

How did she become like that? I am sure one of the most significant ways was through losing her husband so young. Something no one would choose to have happen, something that wasn't of itself good... but that God used for good.

She is a woman who has learned to count her blessings, and who has taught me to do the same. On my list of blessings today is:

- The sun is shining.
- The spring flowers are coming out.
- I have a body that works.
- I haven't got a headache (I always notice it when I have got one, so I try to notice and thank the Lord for days when I haven't!)
- I have a loving family.
- I have precious friends.

- My sister has just sent me a lovely picture of my nephews.
- I have a great boss and brilliant work colleagues.
- I am part of a supportive, encouraging church family.
- I live in a lovely, cosy home.
- I had a safe, easy car journey this morning.
- I've got a very nice cake to eat later!

They are all signs of God's goodness and grace to me today. But even on rainy days when I have a headache, and no cake... and no husband... I can still write down my blessings, hard though that may be. Because whatever I do or don't have, I can always write:

- Jesus loves me, and died for me, and is working for my good today.

And, as I look at that truth, and I ask him to work in my heart through his Spirit, I can even find myself writing down under my list of blessings:

- It's raining.
- I have a headache.
- I don't have any cake.
- I am single.

As God changes our hearts and gives us a right perspective, we can thank God for unlooked-for blessings as well, for unrequested gifts we would never have chosen—including bad weather, ill health, lack of sweet food... and singleness.

Why not prayerfully count all your blessings now?

7. Satisfied in all situations

If you struggle, or have struggled, with being single, you'll know there are certain situations, and certain times of the year, which are particularly hard, and where our hearts are especially susceptible to being deceived.

It's important to recognise that there's nothing wrong with finding things hard; let's be real and honest about how we feel. But the crucial thing is what we then do with our pain and our struggles.

Giving in to self-pity, envy of others, and/or bitterness towards God is a huge danger for all of us—because it is what the devil will encourage our hearts to do. We need to be aware of what is likely to throw us—what the "triggers" are likely to be for us—so that we can take pre-emptive action, speaking truth to our hearts rather than listening to his lies.

Below, I've listed the times I have found (and still find) hard as a single woman—and the mistakes I know I can easily make in those moments, and the truth I need to remind myself of. The triggers may be different for you. But whatever and whenever they are, good questions to ask are:

- How could I be deceived in a Sally-like way or in a Maya-like way in this situation?

- What am I longing for, so that I'm being tempted to look somewhere other than Jesus to find it? How is he in actual fact the answer to that longing?

When friends get engaged

We receive a phone call or text telling us that yet another of our friends is getting married, and once again we get that aching pain in the pit of our stomach. A familiar thought comes into our minds: *Why am I still single? What's wrong with me?*

- *A lie I might listen to:* God doesn't want me to be happy. God hasn't given me a husband because he doesn't really care about me.

- *A Sally-like solution:* Grit my teeth and bear it. Look happy on the surface, while wallowing in my unchallenged envy and resentment underneath.

- *A Maya-like solution:* Conclude that the only way I'll be happy is by finding a guy... so I need to get myself a guy.

- *A truth to tell myself:* God has given me every spiritual blessing in Christ. He chose me before the creation of the world to be his, and to be loved in his sight. He has made me his child, through faith in Jesus (from Ephesians 1 v 3-5). He isn't keeping good things back—I can trust him because of what he has done for me and has given me.

Weddings

There are lots of things that it can be difficult to go to on your own, but when it's a wedding we can feel our lack of husband more keenly than ever. The fact that someone else is getting married and we're not is likely to highlight afresh that we are still single, and may well mean we find ourselves struggling to cope with innocent comments that are made or questions that are asked throughout the day. (At one wedding a lady I had just met asked me who my husband was; I told her that I wasn't married. She then asked me when my baby was due, which was especially surprising as I am a size 10. I don't think I ever wore that dress again!)

- *A lie I might listen to:* Without a husband I am insignificant. Everyone else thinks so—so it must be true.

- *A Sally-like solution:* I'll keep doing my duty until God gives me what I deserve.

- *A Maya-like solution:* I don't like feeling like this. I need to walk down an aisle myself, or at least to have a man on my arm next time I'm invited to a wedding. That's my top priority now.

- *A truth to tell myself:* Whatever else I have, or could have, is worth nothing compared to the surpassing greatness of knowing Christ. He is worth losing anything for. What I most need is what I already have: Jesus (from Philippians 3 v 7-8). Husbands may look perfect on their wedding day, but they aren't. They couldn't satisfy all my longings, now or eternally. Only Jesus can; so I need to turn to him in my heart, not away from him.

When friends have children

I think this can be particularly hard as we approach our forties, and the reality that we might never have our own children begins to hit home. Having children is likely to be something, like marriage, that most of us have longed for and have just expected will happen at some stage. We may find ourselves surrounded by women who seem to talk about their pregnancy, babies or children all the time... which can just feel as if salt is being rubbed into the wound.

- *A lie I might listen to:* I am unfulfilled as a woman if I don't have children.

- *A Sally-like response:* To think I have been a "good girl", and I deserve children a lot more than many of the people God has given children to; I will avoid people who have children.

- *A Maya-like response:* It is my right to have children and I need children, so I will do whatever I can to make sure I get what I "need".

- *A truth to tell myself:* I need to trust in the Lord with all my heart and not rely on my own understanding. As I acknowledge his lordship, he'll guide me on straight paths, whatever they may be (Proverbs 3 v 5-6). Having a child won't fulfil me. If I place all my hopes in having a child, even if I ended up with one I would crush them with my expectations and demands. If I cut myself off from everyone with children, I'll cut myself off from enjoying life as an auntie to church families. I need to delight in the Lord and follow him, and enjoy the children he has given me to know, love and pray for.

Holidays

We may feel that married couples always have each other to go away with; it isn't always straightforward for us as single women. It might not be easy to find people to go away with and to make holiday plans generally. In the back of our minds it's a romantic holiday for two that we ultimately dream of. Any other holiday can feel like second best to us.

- *A lie I might listen to:* I'm all alone.

- *A Sally-like solution:* Not to really value, pursue or invest in any relationships in the church family; to be cold and distant, just going through the motions. After all, I'm passing the time until I "get my husband".

- *A Maya-like solution:* My dream romantic holiday requires me not to be single. Being single means I'm missing out; so I need to get a man.

- *A truth to tell myself:* There is nowhere that I am, that God is not with me through his Spirit. If I go to the heavens, or the depths, or the far side of the sea, God is with me, guiding and holding me (from Psalm 139 v 7-10). I am never alone. When I feel lonely, I need to ask Jesus to make his presence more real to me; not to turn my back on him and seek company elsewhere. And I need to ask him to help me trust that he is right there with me, even when it doesn't feel as though he is.

Christmas

This is one of those times in the year when single women can end up feeling like failures, like sad spinsters who just don't fit in. In our worst moments, we have nothing but the image of how it was "meant to be" in our heads. We picture everyone else's home as including a happy couple, kneeling by the tree, hand in hand on Christmas morning watching their beautiful, grateful, perfectly behaved children opening their presents.

And this pain is only heightened if we know our parents are disappointed that, because we have no children, they have no grandchildren to buy presents for, make Christmas lunch for, and so on.

- *A lie I might listen to:* I don't belong or fit in anywhere.
- *A Sally-like solution:* To refuse offers of hospitality to spend time over Christmas with other families, bitterly thinking: *I don't want pity or charity; I want my own family*

or nothing at all. I decide Christmas will be miserable, and get on with fulfilling my prediction.

- *A Maya-like solution:* To numb myself to the pain—look to the world's answers to how to have a good time, find comfort, or feel better: get drunk, get high, sleep with someone. Anything that makes me feel that I belong.

- *A truth to tell myself:* When Jesus was told his family were looking for him, he said his real mothers and brothers were those who do God's will (from Mark 3 v 32-35). I belong in a family that is loving, that looks out for me, that welcomes me, and that I will be blessed by as I love and look out for them. I belong in my church.

The grass really isn't greener

Ultimately, the big lie which lies behind each of these is: *You are missing out.*

As single women, I think it's so easy for us to take as a simple fact that life is happier, easier, and better if you're married. The grass is greener over there (and there's a husband to mow it).

The Bible tells us, and experience shows us when we are able to think clearly about it, that marriage and singleness are both good and both hard; and that they are different good and different hard. But I find it very easy to focus only on the good bits of marriage, and the bad bits of singleness. As I do so, the whisper in my heart becomes a shout: *You are missing out.*

And when that happens, we need to reorient our hearts. This happens as we do three things:

1. Mine the Scriptures

Come to the Scriptures with your personal situation in mind. In other words, without allowing your circumstances to dominate what you take away from God's word, as you look at a narrative or doctrine, ask how it might be able to encourage you. For instance, take Hagar, Abraham's slave-girl who was shunned and shut out by his wife Sarah, after (at Sarah's suggestion) she bore him a son. Genesis 16 v 1-16 shows us that God is a God who sees the lonely, struggling woman, and ensures that she has what she needs. The psalms reveal to us that God is ready to listen to our struggles; that we can be honest with him, and bring our pain to him. We see Jesus stopping to speak to the hopeless, bleeding woman. And countless other stories and truths remind us of God's character, and that he knows us, cares for us, is with us, and is being good to us in our situations.

2. Pray to God

As the writers of the psalms so often do, it is good for us to pour our hearts out to God, to tell him exactly how we're feeling and ask him to help us. We can ask Jesus, who knows us completely and understands all our sorrows and joys, to help us believe what is true, to help us keep trusting him, and to comfort and strengthen us by his Spirit. When we miss the practical support and companionship of a husband, let's ask Jesus to help our hearts believe that he is the Husband who truly fulfils what we most need.

3. Value Christian friends

Our friendships with both single and married women are so important, and are such a precious gift from God. The closer we are to each other, and the more honest we are with each other, the more clearly we will see that no outward circumstances, including our marital status, can ever in themselves make us happy. One of the reasons I am extremely grateful for the close married friends I have is that they have let me see, first hand, that marriage is far from the perfect picture of love and harmony that I, as a single woman, might imagine it to be. In these friendships I get to see both that marriage is good... but also that it is hard. The relationships we have with other women, married and single, are wonderful gifts from God, which we should really value and make the most of.

I need these things to remind me of the truth about God, and life, and marriage and singleness; and I have also found I need to avoid some things which undermine that truth. Watching romantic comedies tends to generate a dissatisfaction in me that wasn't there before I watched the film. Although I love that kind of film, I have noticed that my heart is usually not in a good place after watching one, so I would be wiser not to. Or thinking about ex-boyfriends and wondering what they're up to now invariably leads me to wondering what might have been, whether they think about me, whether I'd have been happier if we'd stayed together... and that unsettles my heart. So I need to catch myself at the beginning of that thought process, and consciously do something else or think about something else. I've found one thing that works for me is simply to listen to some music full of gospel truths. Another is to identify upcoming trigger points and ask a couple of friends to pray for me, and tell them what I will probably need reminding of that day or the next day, so that they can send me a text or ring me up and know how they can help me.

Writing your own conclusion

No two people's characters are the same. No two people's circumstances are the same. We all face, enjoy, and wrestle with a unique combination of the two. So in a way, only you can know how the gospel truths I've written about apply to you. Only you can know whether and how you're tempted to live like Sally or Maya; and whether and how you're trying just to be better at seeing singleness as a gift.

Only you can know when and how you need to bask in the Son, enjoying knowing and being loved and cared for by him. But the questions that it's helpful to ask, and the truths we need to remember, are the same for all of us:

Questions to ask yourself

1. What is my heart telling me about myself in this situation?

2. What is my heart telling me about God in this situation?

3. What do I know to be true about God that speaks to me about this situation?

4. In the light of the truths I know about God, can I identify what lies my heart is telling me?

5. Can I see what the "hook" under the "bait" of the lies is?

6. What promises of God do I need to hold onto in this situation (look at the big picture, not just your immediate situation)?

7. What can I thank God for?

Truths to remember

1. God loves you more that you can even begin to imagine!

2. God knows what is best for you.

3. God will do what is best for you, as you look to him and trust him.

4. He knows how you feel and is with you in your pain.

5. You are his treasured possession. He has ransomed, healed, restored and forgiven you.

6. You have the glorious hope of eternal life; you are not missing out on what you most need in life, even if you remain single all your life.

7. The Lord has prepared good works for you to do in the situation that you are in. He will equip you to do them and bless you as you do them in his strength, in his name and for his glory.

I don't know how this book has challenged or changed you. I hope it's comforted and encouraged and excited you, too. But one thing that's worth remembering is that change doesn't happen overnight. None of us can flick a switch which transforms our thinking, far less our feelings. It takes time to become women who are single and satisfied.

So, wherever you're at in your relationship with Jesus, and however you're feeling about being single, remember this. God doesn't want you to have a bitter heart, sitting in church but not loving and joyful. He doesn't want you to have a torn heart, living in rebellion against him and pretending that's fine. He wants more than a cracked cistern for you; much, much more. He wants you to know the joy and happiness and security of living water. That's why he's given you the desires of your heart.

That's why he's given you his Son.

Appendix: What's wrong with sex outside marriage?

Sex is a good thing, the Bible says. After God created the first man and woman, and placed them in a flawless world, we read:

> A man leaves his father and mother and is united to his wife,
> and they become one flesh. (Genesis 2 v 24)

Sex is a good gift from God, made to be enjoyed. And it is made to be enjoyed within marriage between one man and one woman.

Our culture, and sometimes our hearts, say that this is totally unreasonable. It sounds harsh and restrictive to say to anyone who isn't married that they shouldn't be having sex. It can't be right, we're told, to deny or suppress those natural desires that we have, and miss out on something that is so good.

We are frequently told, through all sorts of media, that sex is just a physical thing; as long as you are being "safe", you are free to, and should, just go for it. But God says that his good gift of sex is not just a physical thing. It's far more, far better, than that. To quote some great philosophers of the 1990s, the Spice Girls... when sex is involved, "tonight is the night when two become one". A man and a woman "become one flesh". Something much deeper and much more significant happens when two people have sex, even if we deny it. If we say that's not true, we are deceiving ourselves by believing the lie the world tells us.

In so many films, we watch two carefree, beautiful people flirting with each other, sleeping together (often, you don't actually see that bit—you just see them kissing, and then suddenly it's dawn!), and then going their separate ways; all is fine—it was just a physical thing. They both got something out of it and then moved on.

But in reality that is not how it is; that is not how God has made us. When we give ourselves to someone else, we can't just "move on" unaffected, because we have become one with that person.

But isn't there a difference between this kind of casual, one-night-stand sex, and sex in a long-term relationship? We all know couples who aren't married, but who have lived together for years, and love each other very much. Why is sex wrong in that context? But let's be clear: if a couple are not married, they have not made a truly life-long commitment to each other, in public, for everyone to see, to know about, and to help them hold to. Both are reserving the right to walk away. Outside marriage, at least one partner is saying to the other: *I love you today, but I may not love you tomorrow. I am here today, but I can't guarantee that I will be in a decade. My love is not truly unconditional.*

Sex is the total, ultimate self-giving, in the most utterly complete and vulnerable way; and God says it is to be enjoyed only between two people who have committed themselves to each other, who have given themselves to one another and who are in a permanent, exclusive, marriage relationship. Anything outside of that is not part of God's good plan for sex—and is therefore wrong.

The New Testament is full of passages calling us as Christians to be the people God has made us to be—not by urging us to try harder, but by reminding us of who we are now that we know Jesus:

> Since then, you have been raised with Christ, set your hearts
> on things above, where Christ is, seated at the right hand of
> God. Set your minds on things above, not on earthly things.
> For you died, and your life is now hidden with Christ in God.
> When Christ, who is your life, appears, then you also will
> appear with him in glory. (Colossians 3 v 1-4)

As those who belong to God, we are to choose to set our hearts and minds on "things above"—that is, on what God says (what is good and right and true) and not on "earthly things"—that is, on what the world tells us (which is not good and not right and not true). And we are to live with our eyes fixed on that glorious future day, when we will be with him for ever. On that day, we will know we have not missed out by living God's way. Until then, Paul says:

> Put to death, therefore, whatever belongs to your earthly
> nature: sexual immorality, impurity, lust. (v 5)

Sexual immorality is Bible shorthand for any sexual act outside the context of marriage between a man and a woman. If you are a Christian, whatever you have done in the past—whatever sins you have committed (including sexual sins of any kind)—has all been wonderfully forgiven. You are free to live the way God designed you to, to enjoy knowing him, to have your heart captivated by Jesus and how he loves you. You are free not to run after what the world says you must experience.

Contrary to what our culture constantly tells us, we don't need to have sex. There are many people who have had, or are having, sex, and yet still find themselves feeling insecure, heartbroken, lonely, or deeply damaged. There is no one who knows and trusts Jesus who needs to feel like that. Our society often suggests that having sex is what we need. It isn't. Jesus is.

Appendix: What's wrong with marrying a non-Christian anyway?

It's helpful to start by thinking about what it means to be a Christian; what it means to belong to Christ. He is not a hobby, he is our hearts' Ruler. He is not something we like, he's the someone we love most. (For more on why he deserves this position in our lives, chapter five goes into more detail.)

This means that our faith is not one thing in our lives among many—it's the centre of our lives, the focus of everything in it. Christianity isn't something we do, like a book club or keep fit class; it is something we are. It makes a total difference to us.

This is why Paul uses some quite strong language in a letter to a first-century Greek church:

> Do not be yoked together with unbelievers. For what do righteousness and wickedness have in common? Or what fellowship can light have with darkness? ... What does a believer have in common with an unbeliever?
>
> (2 Corinthians 6 v 14, 16a)

At first, Paul's words may sound harsh; but what he is wanting to stress is two things. First, that Christians and non-Christians are totally different. As Christians, whatever else we have in common with a non-Christian, we have a completely opposite attitude to the most important person—Jesus. What drives us, what we trust in, how we approach our hopes and fears and decisions and difficulties, is as different as light and dark.

Secondly, Paul makes the point that the people who are closest to us have a huge influence on us. The image he uses is of being "yoked", like two oxen who are linked together to pull a plough. Being yoked together means they move in the same direction, at the same pace. Paul's point is that we tend to become like those we spend time with; we pick up mannerisms and expressions they use, even when we're not trying to or don't want to! When I moved to Sevenoaks eleven years ago, I never used the word "folk". But it's one of my boss's favourite words—and, someone pointed out to me recently, I now seem to use it all the time.

In 2 Corinthians, Paul is talking about close relationships, not just marriage. But there's no closer relationship between two people than husband and wife. So while Paul isn't *only* talking about marriage, he certainly *is* talking about it.

Let's face it, it is not easy to love Christ more than ourselves, or more than other things that our hearts are prone to think will give us what we think we need in life. If we marry, we're going to need our husband's help. And it's unfair to expect a non-Christian husband to do that, because he can't. With the best will in the world, he's going to hinder us. A man who is not a Christian, who is in the dark, just isn't able actively to encourage me to look to Jesus, trust him, grow in my love for him and live for him. At best, I will struggle in my faith. At worst, I will give up on it.

We need a husband who understands that he isn't, and who doesn't want to be, our greatest love—a husband whose greatest desire for us is that we will love Jesus more and more. It will always cause tension in a marriage if a husband doesn't understand, and so doesn't want us to love Jesus more than them.

And it's not just our own Christian lives that are worth thinking about. If I ever have children, what I will most want for them is to know Jesus, to enjoy living for him now and look forward to living with him for ever. If my husband isn't a Christian, that won't be what he most wants for them. How can I expect him to encourage my children to have a faith that he doesn't have? What will he tell them about why we are here, what matters and where we are going? What will I do when my child announces they'll stay home with dad instead of coming to church with me?

I know lots of women who live with this pain, especially as their children get older. Many end up bringing (in some cases dragging) their children to church on their own; often their children want to stay at home with dad. A number of women in that situation have told me that they feel torn apart.

The statistics support their experience. A Swiss study in 2000 found that, when both parents regularly attend church, 33% of their children will do so into adulthood. When it is only the mother who goes to church, that number drops to 2%. Of course, the Holy Spirit isn't restricted by statistics, and can save anyone from any family background! But it's worth asking: Why would I put myself, and any future children I have, into a situation where I'll either have to ignore the truths of the Bible in order to feel comfortable, or feel torn apart because I know they are true?

Finally, it's actually not good for a non-Christian man to be married to a Christian. It's worth asking: What is best for the man who I'd like to marry—to be married to me, or to have a living faith in Jesus? Non-Christians in relationships with Christians are under great pressure to convert. Many find that pressure too great, with devastating consequences for both them and their girlfriend or wife. But even if they do make a profession of faith, it's very hard for them to be sure that they really do love Jesus and want to please him, rather than that they really love their girl and want to please her by convincing her, and themselves, that they love Jesus.

When it comes to this issue, which is so emotional and sometimes painful for us, we want clear proof that the Bible says: *This is not ok.* We want a verse that says: *You shall not marry a non-Christian* or we won't believe that this is what God wants for us. And the Bible is pretty clear when it says, in the context of a widow finding a new husband, "he must belong to the Lord" (1 Corinthians 7 v 39). But in fact individual verses or commands won't ultimately help us with this. We need to be convinced, and so believe in our hearts, that whatever situation will help me love Jesus and live for him more has got to be the best situation for me. That might be being married to a Christian. Or it might be not to be married. But it simply can't be choosing to marry someone who doesn't know or love Jesus.

And this is all relevant when we come to think about dating. It's easy to think that going out with a non-Christian is fine—it's not marriage. I know from personal experience, though, what a painful path this is to go down. There's a good chance we'll fall in love with the man we're dating (otherwise we wouldn't go out with him!). When that happens, our heart will more and more listen to how we feel, and look to the man we are in love with, instead of listening to God's truth and looking to Jesus.

If you go out with someone and one or both of you fall in love, it can only end in two ways: breaking up, or marriage. When a Christian woman goes out with a non-Christian, the first means heartache for them or their boyfriend (or both); the second means disobeying the God who loves us enough to die for us. Neither is a happy ending.

When asked what the greatest commandment is, Jesus said:

> Love the Lord your God with all your heart and with all your soul and with all your mind. This is the first and greatest commandment. (Mark 12 v 30)

How are you and I going to do that? By putting God first in our lives. How do you and I do *that*?! By trusting and obeying all that he says in his word, and not letting anything or anyone hinder our relationship with him. And by believing that God is good, and he knows what is best for all his children.

Appendix: Helping single friends

You may have read this book because you have single friends and you want to support them, encourage them, and avoid saying or doing things which are unhelpful to them. If that's you, thanks for taking the time to read this! These ten do's and don'ts aren't an exhaustive list (you could ask your friends what would help, and definitely not help, them)—but they are things that I have found really helpful and unhelpful.

Ways to be helpful for your single friends:

1. *Be honest with them about the challenges as well as the joys of marriage.* It is obvious to most single women what the joys of marriage are, so it is really helpful for you to let your single friends see the reality of some of the day-to-day challenges up close, which should happen naturally if you share your lives with them. This doesn't mean being critical of or disloyal towards your husband, or moaning about your blessings (like children). It does mean not presenting your marriage as a place of perfect happiness. Single women do need to be reminded that real marriage is not like it sometimes looks from the outside!

2. *Make and value your single friends as part of your family / your children's lives.* It is a great joy and a privilege to be an "auntie" who can just pop round to friends for tea sometimes, help with bath/bed time, babysit or just hang out with the family. Single friends who don't have children of their own can be a real blessing to you... as well as you being a blessing to them.

3. *Challenge them (graciously and lovingly) if they are wallowing in self-pity about being single.* It is not helpful to let your single friends constantly feel sorry for themselves and complain to

you that life is not fair. It may be difficult to challenge them from the position of "happily married", but if you are a close friend, this is a way of really loving them and helping them to grow.

4. *Pray for them. And pray primarily that they will grow to love and live for the Lord Jesus more and more.* Rather than just praying that the Lord will give your friend a husband, pray for them to be growing more like Christ, and for you both to be making the most of every opportunity to bring glory to the Lord in the unique situations he has given you. And you could tell them that this is what you are praying for them.

5. *Think about what photos you put in your living room or kitchen.* I love it when I go round to married friends' homes and see not only (or even) their wedding photos, pictures of their children and whole-family holiday snaps, but also photos of other families and friends (sometimes including me!). This reminds me that "family" doesn't just mean the nuclear family, that I am not on my own, and that as a Christian I am part of a wonderful wider family. It means I'm not being reminded of what I don't have, but of what I do have.

Things likely to be unhelpful:

1. *Trying to set them up with someone.* This gives the impression that you think their singleness is a problem that needs to be fixed, and that until they meet someone they are just passing time until life can really begin.

2. *Asking them if they've met anyone yet.* If this is often the topic of conversation, it can encourage your single friend to focus on this above all else, and to feel incomplete until she meets someone.

3. *Asking them why they are still single.* It amazes me how many people, especially married men, seem to think that this is

a good question to ask! They usually say something like: "So why is a lovely girl like you still single?" Although I'm sure it's not meant to, it comes across as patronising and is embarrassing... and how are you meant to answer?!

4. *Saying things like: "I'm sure the Lord has someone for you".* I know this is usually said to be kind to someone who is struggling with singleness and is desperately hoping that a husband will come along. But you can't be sure—God may, in his good and loving plans, not have someone lined up for me, and that needs to be OK. Encourage your friend to keep finding fulfilment in their relationship with Jesus, and trusting him in the situation they are in now.

5. *Only doing things with other married couples/families.* I know of married couples who are nervous of inviting single people to come round along with married couples, because they think the single people will find it too hard. But do at least invite them and see! I so appreciate being included in plans made by married friends, and really value the friendship and gentle teasing (not about being single!) of some of my friends' husbands, who are like brothers to me, who look out for me and support and encourage me.

Real faith: This may be a difficult truth to live by

Gabrielle's story:

I'm twenty-two and single, and for me singleness is one of the areas where what I believe about God has to really dictate how I feel.

When I was younger, I think I did hold an assumption that I would, at some point, get married; it seemed almost like the default progression. But as I've grown in my faith, I've realised that marriage isn't a given. If I really believe that the point of life is to glorify God and to enjoy him for ever, then I need to praise God for whichever circumstances he brings me, whether that turns out to be singleness or marriage.

Really gripping hold of that truth means that whatever happens, God is sovereign, good and deserving of glory. This is a very easy thing to say, but I know that, one day, it may be a very difficult truth to live by.

There does seem to be a bit of an assumption about marriage for young, single, Christian women. I think a lot of it is found in how we talk about purity. We're encouraged to "wait for our husbands", to "stay pure for marriage", to prepare ourselves to be godly wives and mothers. But that's all based on the assumption that we'll get married! Most of us will, but some of us won't, leaving the question: "Well, what am I remaining pure *for*, then?" I've found it really helpful to realise that the finishing line for the pursuit of purity isn't marriage, it's growing closer to God. I need to remember that I am not waiting for a guaranteed husband; he may not arrive.

I find it really helpful when I get the chance to spend time with older women, both married and single, to see how they live out their faith in everyday ways. It's good for me to see what godly singleness looks like, and to watch how husbands and wives relate to one another. But my experience—and the experience of a lot of my friends—is that we tend to have a lot of young, single friends, and not a lot of friends from other ages within our churches. I know I need to develop relationships with other older Christians—if you're one of those, and you're reading this, young, single women need your guidance, support and wisdom—please invite us round for a cup of tea!

It is sometimes hard being single as someone in her early twenties. This time of life is full of decision-making: what type of career to pursue, where to live, which church to commit to, how to serve, and so on. I don't have somebody to make those big decisions with; someone to share that responsibility with. Of course, I can pray and speak with Christian friends, but sometimes I want somebody to live life with. I would like to be married! But having said that, and despite those difficulties, being 22 and single is great! It's a time for me to increase in devotedness to the Lord, to focus on loving and serving his church, and to learn to make the most of the advantages of being single, whether that's for a period, or for a lifetime.

Real faith: I only imagined myself being married

Brenda's story:

I can say with all honesty that today I feel content in my singleness. I haven't always been able to say that!

In fact as a young girl, I only imagined my older self as being married with children. In my teenage years, when my friends and I began to experience opposite-sex relationships, I found myself desiring marriage in my future. By the time I was in my 20s, marriage had become something I really, really wanted, and thought I couldn't live without. The need to find a partner began to feel a little desperate.

Then I met a lovely older Christian woman. She was 36 years old, and single... and she seemed happy. It was a shock to me. I couldn't think of any reason why she wasn't married. She was great. But she was single. Why would God do this to her? How could she accept it and be happy? For the first time in my life, I contemplated the possibility of staying single. I couldn't really imagine it, and I didn't want to. Surely I would be lonely, depressed and miserable, even as a Christian? The thought scared me.

At this time, most of my friends were getting married, including my closest friends. I was a bridesmaid six times in five years. Thankfully I didn't feel any bitterness, like some single girls I knew did. I enjoyed going through the life changes with these newly married friends.

Actually, I think their continued friendship is one of the main things that has helped me in my singleness. They were open about their marriage relationship—about the good things and the hard things. This gave me a realistic view of marriage. As a single woman, it's so easy to romanticise the idea of marriage.

I've needed to be reminded often of the reality that it's just normal, with blessings and joys and struggles and frustrations. As these friends began to have babies, and I continued to be a part of their lives, I saw how tiring and draining children could be. Yes, there were special moments, and I loved being involved, but at the end of the day I could go home and enjoy the peace, quiet and simplicity I have as a single person.

Of course there have been struggles, and probably there always will be. I find it hard that married friends will often invite me to things at the last minute, as though single people just sit around at home, waiting and hoping for an invitation. But I plan to do things in advance, so that I'm not sitting at home alone.

Another unhelpful thing married friends do sometimes is ask if there is anyone I'm interested in or like at the moment. The reason this is frustrating is because if there was someone like that, I'd have told them—they're my friends! But it also feeds the misconception that being married is better than being single. I need encouragement in my singleness, not help to get married!

Having good single friends has been a great help; in many ways, these friends have become real companions in life. We are in similar life situations, being single, and so can do things like go on holidays together and spend days off together. We can help each other to enjoy the blessings of singleness. There are so many things we get to enjoy as single people, which we can so easily overlook when we long for a different situation.

The greatest help of all, of course, has been the closest of friends— Jesus. He has really helped me to notice and appreciate these things, and enjoy them. And I believe God has given me a real contentment in my singleness. I am now 36 years old—the age that single friend was when I met her. And I am like her—single and content. I could never have imagined it! I really do thank God for it.

Real faith: I was a Christian, but still gay

Emily's story:

I started noticing that I was different at 11. My friends were noticing boys; I was noticing other girls. I had no idea at that stage, but gradually over the next few years I realised that I was gay. I worried about it, so I kept quiet.

Then we went on a school trip when I was 15, and met some girls from another school. I really fancied one of those girls, and she liked me, so we got together. That meant I kind of had to tell people! My friends and family were all very supportive. And that was it, really—I was gay. I wasn't promiscuous, but I was active.

I went off to university to study drama quite happy with who I was. I was fairly involved in the LGBT scene at uni. If someone had told me that it was wrong, I'd have told them they were wrong—that you can't deny who you are or how you feel, you can't hide or change it; so how can it be wrong?

My road to becoming a Christian began through a friend on my drama course. We went on tour together in the summer at the end of my first year, and part of getting to know her better meant getting to know her as a Christian. I'd never before met someone of my age who was a genuine Christian.

She lent me her Bible, and I read the Gospels. Part way through, I had a moment where I suddenly felt I needed to pray—so I said to God: "I don't know who you are or what you are, but hello, what do I do now?"

I started going to church and meeting more and more Christians. At some point, the issue of homosexuality came up. I slowly understood that I couldn't be both a Christian and actively gay; but Jesus was really exciting, so I carried on going along. And in one sermon, the main point was: Do you want to be at Jesus' heavenly banquet? And I thought: "Yes I do!" I started following Christ.

So then I was a Christian, but still gay. I remember there was one point where I thought: *If I believe all the other things there is no way I can deny what the Bible says about sex, that it should be within a marriage of a man and woman. I can't ignore that just because I don't like it.*

But it was hard, very hard. I was walking along once and I just burst into tears, in the street, because I had a sudden realisation of: *That's it, I'm never going to be with anyone, ever. I'm never going to have a human, earthly relationship.*

I've often asked myself why I didn't back away from Christianity at that point. It was because the joy that I'd experienced knowing Jesus, being saved and changed by him, was greater than any joy I'd ever experienced from being with someone. I knew it was never going to be easy, but the alternative was turning my back on Jesus. And there was no way I wanted to do that.

So I still fancied women, but I didn't act on it. You can't deny your sexual preference, but what you can do is to say no to giving in to it and acting on it.

Then a couple of years on, when I was at drama school, I realised that I really liked a guy there. And I thought: *Hang on, that's not supposed to happen!* Slowly, I realised that God had changed my sexual preference. That was his choice; it doesn't happen to everyone, and I wasn't expecting it to happen to me at all. I'd prayed for the strength to deal with what I'd been given and how I felt, and his choice was to change me.

So now I'm straight, and single—and it's much harder! As a non-practising gay Christian, you know that that is it: you're single. You know where you stand, other Christians support you, and no one says things like: "I'm sure someone will come along for you". But now I know that singleness may not be forever for me—and I have to try to remember that singleness or marriage might be God's plan for me, and that either is good. That's hard in a different way.

Real faith: My marriage ended in a divorce court

Lin's story:

When I was younger, I was more focused on going to university and choosing a career path than getting married. If the subject ever came up in discussion with friends, I would say that any future partner would have to be intelligent, caring, and someone I could talk to, share my inmost thoughts and feelings with—a "soul-mate".

So, when I was at university and I did meet that very clever young man with whom I was able to share all those inmost feelings, someone I could look up to, trust, and confide in, we became friends and fell in love. We were married, had successful careers, bought a house, were very happy, and decided to have a baby to complete the picture. My husband's career was progressing fast and took us abroad for four years, where we both worked hard, enjoyed the life, and had our second child.

When the time came to relocate back to England, I returned first with our two children in order to set up our new home and settle our elder daughter into school. This left my husband on his own, open to temptations which he didn't resist.

I tried to put the broken pieces of the marriage back together again. I tried for twelve years, but the betrayal and the lies continued. My marriage ended in a divorce court.

But during the last, dark months of my marriage, there was a glimmer of light. The mother of one of my daughter's school-friends is a Christian. One day she saw something was wrong, came over and sat in my car, and offered to pray for me. She invited me to a course at her church. I was not a Christian and had always rejected any approach made by Christians. So

I was amazed as I heard myself, through my tears, accept the invitation.

That was the start of my journey to faith. I discovered that Jesus could be trusted, wouldn't deceive or lie, and would never turn his back on me and run away. I wanted him in my life, so I became a Christian, joined a loving and caring church, and got baptised.

I now live as a single woman again, but I am never alone. God said: "[I] will never leave you or forsake you" (Deuteronomy 31 v 6).

There have been difficult moments: coming face to face with my ex-husband for the first time (four years after our divorce) when his mother was very ill; at our younger daughter's graduation ceremony; and then with his new wife at my mother-in-law's funeral. But each time, I sensed God's support and presence, his strength and protection.

Christmas has probably been the most difficult time of year to manage (especially because I'm not one of the world's most gifted cooks!). When the children were younger, I would take them to stay in a hotel. Now they are adults, I've learned either to invite others to come and join in the preparations and festivities, or to swallow my pride and accept other people's generous invitations to spend Christmas with them.

I've never considered seeking a new husband—and I used to find it immensely irritating when someone kept telling me to go online and sign up to a Christian dating organisation! I know that if God wants me to marry again, he will provide me with a man of his own choosing, in his own timing.

I don't feel bitter and twisted; gradually God has been teaching me to forgive. Yes, there can be sad days, so I tell myself to remember all the blessings my God has given me through my life: the loving parents, the privileges of education, the happy years I did experience during my marriage, the two beautiful children given as gifts to be cared for from that marriage, Jesus coming into my life, and all the things he is teaching me.

I know that I am loved, and I am cared for. I know that God has promised: "My unfailing love for you will not be shaken" (Isaiah 54 v 10).

Real faith: My widowhood is not out of his control

Jean's story:

In marriage, two become one. For me that happened to Robert and me in February 1970. Because every individual is unique, two unique individuals make a unique relationship with each other and with God in marriage.

Separating the white and yolk of an egg is easy at the start, but once they are scrambled, it's impossible. In the same way you cannot just return back to life as a single when marriage ends. This was hard to grasp when in 2003, aged 55, Robert died of a brain tumour. I was not really married. I was not really single. I was sort of both—I was a widow.

Robert just wasn't there anymore: to lean on as my lover, as the father of our children, as my friend, supporter, wise counsellor, corrector and encourager. We had been apart before, like when he went away on business. Then he was just a telephone call away. This was different; now I felt as if I was completely on my own.

During the last year of Robert's life, when I knew he was going to be taken away, my prayer to God was that I would not be bitter and turn against him. But I was left not knowing who I was. I felt as if I had lost my identity. During his last months, I asked Robert if he ever wondered: *Why me?* His death seemed so premature. His reply was a challenge to me. "Why not me?" he replied.

He would sometimes say in that last precious year together: "You have the harder task, of carrying on without me, but God will help you". When aloneness floods over me, these words are comforting. Psalm 139 v 2 says of God: "You know when I sit down and when I rise up". God knows every detail of my life. My widowhood is not out of his control.

When you are married, it is very easy to turn to your husband first and to God second. As a widow, crying out to God for help in all the everyday situations of life, I've learned that God is faithful in his promises to care for the widow. Like all single people, I have difficult times when I wonder if God is hard of hearing! But over time his words have become more real and alive to me. He provides just what I need, and when I need it.

Singleness feels harder in a world that promotes couples. The saying "You can feel lonely in a crowd" becomes reality when you walk into church or a party alone. Then I remember that God is not unfaithful to any of his promises and he promised to care for the widow.

When you become a widow, you have to re-learn all of the coping mechanisms. You are initially seen as on the marriage market, as well-meaning friends parade all their single male friends before you. Even my parents thought that, as I was fairly young and intelligent, I would be married within a year. I felt as if I had disappointed them. I have realised that when I was married, I too made comments to others that showed a lack of understanding of what it is like to be single.

Many times I have wanted to tell God that I could serve better if I were married. In difficult situations, whether helping others or giving hospitality, I have wished for that confidential listening ear, for someone who understood. But Paul is quite clear in 1 Corinthians 7 that to be single is better. And over the last ten years, being a widow has given me many opportunities where God has been able to use me.

I think of Robert every day. But little by little, I am learning to say: "God, what do you want me to do, and how can I handle this?"

I think it was the Queen Mother who said about her years of widowhood: "It does not get any better; you just get better at it." I know that with God's help this becomes true.

Thank you...

... to the church family and staff team at St Nicholas, Sevenoaks, for all your support and encouragement while I have worked on this book.

... to Agnes B, Bex C, Helen C, Rosie D, Anna R, Sarah R, Cara S, Jean S, Rachel T, Lin W, Helen T, Elizabeth P, Emily A, Kara C, Cherie H, Kaylyn C, Emily D and Colleen G for reading a draft of the book through and giving really helpful feedback. I am so grateful for all your wisdom and insight.

... to those who kindly allowed their personal testimonies to be included in this book.

... to Margaret Rizza for letting me retreat to your lovely place in Deal to write.

... to my editor, Carl Laferton, for all your encouragement and support. I have been greatly surprised and hugely impressed by how insightful you are when it comes to knowing the mind of the average Christian single woman! Your help has been invaluable.

... to my parents and sister, John, Eileen and Jo, for your on-going love and support in all that I do.

... to the wise and godly single women that the Lord has put into my life at various stages, who have been wonderful examples to me of what it looks like to be truly "single and satisfied".

Other books in the **How to** series

Compared to her...
Sophie de Witt

This warm, real and compelling book introduces women to the little-known but commonly-suffered "Compulsive Comparison Syndrome". Sophie shows how CCS causes envy, despair, pride and superiority; explains its causes; reveals how the gospel message treats it; and shows how women can move beyond it to live a life of true, lasting contentment.

"Accessible, jargon-free, and dealing with a struggle that women are very prone to. This is a really helpful book."

Kathy Keller, co-author of "The Meaning of Marriage"

"I started this book assuming it was written for other women. Within a few pages, I had recognised myself in what Sophie was describing. This is a book every woman should read."

Elspeth Pitt, women's worker at St Helen's Bishopsgate, London

Look out for...

- **Serving without sinking:** How to serve Christ and keep your joy *by John Hindley*

- **Eternity changes everything:** How to live now in light of your future *by Stephen Witmer*

Order from your local Good Book website:

UK & Europe: www.thegoodbook.co.uk • US & Canada: www.thegoodbook.com
Australia: www.thegoodbook.com.au • New Zealand: www.thegoodbook.co.nz

Also available from **thegoodbook**
COMPANY

PASSION

HOW CHRIST'S FINAL DAY
CHANGES YOUR EVERY DAY

The cross of Jesus is the centre of human history, and the centre of the Christian faith. And so it should dominate our view of ourselves, our future... and our present.

But does it? And how should it? Mike McKinley follows Luke's account of the final day of Jesus Christ's life on earth. See the hope and the anguish; the joy and the pain; the treachery, desertion, torture and the final heartbreaking, lifebringing death.

Whether you are exploring Christianity, new to faith, or have been following Jesus for years, discover how Christ's Passion changes your heart and challenges your life, transforming not just your last day, but your every day.

Mike McKinley is pastor of Guilford Baptist Church in Virginia, and the author of *"Did the devil make me do it?"* and *"Am I really a Christian?"*.

"A gripping, heartwarming read"
William Taylor, Rector of St Helen's Bishopsgate, London

thegoodbook
COMPANY

thegoodbook
COMPANY
Opening up the Bible

At The Good Book Company, we are dedicated to helping Christians and local churches grow. We believe that God's growth process always starts with hearing clearly what he has said to us through his timeless word—the Bible.

Ever since we opened our doors in 1991, we have been striving to produce resources that honour God in the way the Bible is used. We have grown to become an international provider of user-friendly resources to the Christian community, with believers of all backgrounds and denominations using our Bible studies, books, evangelistic resources, DVD-based courses and training events.

We want to equip ordinary Christians to live for Christ day by day, and churches to grow in their knowledge of God, their love for one another, and the effectiveness of their outreach.

Call us for a discussion of your needs or visit one of our local websites for more information on the resources and services we provide.

UK & Europe: www.thegoodbook.co.uk
US & Canada: www.thegoodbook.com
Australia: www.thegoodbook.com.au
New Zealand: www.thegoodbook.co.nz

UK & Europe: 0333 123 0880
US & Canada: 866 244 2165
Australia: (02) 6100 4211
New Zealand (+64) 3 343 1990